Michael Winterbottom

BRITISH
FILM
MAKERS

Manchester University Press

already published

Anthony Asquith TOM RYALL

Roy Ward Baker GEOFF MAYER

Sydney Box ANDREW SPICEr

Jack Clayton NEIL SINYARD

Lance Comfort BRIAN MCFARLANE

Terence Davies WENDY EVERETT

Terence Fisher PETER HUTCHINGS

Launder and Gilliat BRUCE BABINGTON

Derek Jarman ROWLAND WYMER

Mike Leigh TONY WHITEHEAD

Joseph Losey COLIN GARDNER

Carol Reed PETER WILLIAM EVANS

Michael Reeves BENJAMIN HALLIGAN

Karel Reisz COLIN GARDNER

J. Lee Thompson STEVE CHIBNALL

Michael Winterbottom

BRIAN McFARLANE *and*

DEANE WILLIAMS

Manchester University Press

MANCHESTER AND NEW YORK

distributed exclusively in the USA by Palgrave Macmillan

The right of Brian McFarlane and Deane Williams to be identified as the authors
of this work has been asserted by them in accordance with the Copyright, Designs
and Patents Act 1988.

Published by Manchester University Press
Oxford Road, Manchester M13 9NR, UK
and Room 400, 175 Fifth Avenue, New York, NY 10010, USA
www.manchesteruniversitypress.co.uk

Distributed exclusively in the USA by
Palgrave, 175 Fifth Avenue, New York, NY 10010, USA

Distributed exclusively in Canada by
UBC Press, University of British Columbia, 2029 West Mall,
Vancouver, BC, Canada V6T 1Z2

British Library Cataloguing-in-Publication Data
A catalogue record for this book is available from the British Library

Library of Congress Cataloging-in-Publication Data applied for

ISBN 978 0 7190 7422 6 *hardback*

First published 2009

18 17 16 15 14 13 12 11 10 09   10 9 8 7 6 5 4 3 2 1

Typeset in Scala with Meta display
by Koinonia, Manchester
Printed in Great Britain
by the MPG Books Group

For our partners, Anna Williams
and Geraldine McFarlane, with love

Contents

List of plates

Series editors' foreword

The aim of this series is to present in lively, authoritative volumes a guide to those film-makers who have made British cinema a rewarding but still under-researched branch of world cinema. The intention is to provide books which are up-to-date in terms of information and critical approach, but not bound to any one theoretical methodology. Though all books in the series will have certain elements in common – comprehensive filmographies, annotated bibliographies, appropriate illustration – the actual critical tools employed will be the responsibility of the individual authors.

Nevertheless, an important recurring element will be a concern for how the oeuvre of each film-maker does or does not fit certain critical and industrial contexts, as well as for the wider social contexts which helped to shape not just that particular film-maker but the course of British cinema at large.

Although the series is director-orientated, the editors believe that reference to a variety of stances and contexts is more likely to reconceptualise and reappraise the phenomenon of British cinema as a complex, shifting field of production. All the texts in the series will engage in detailed discussion of major works of the film-makers involved, but they all consider as well the importance of other key collaborators, of studio organisation, of audience reception, of recurring themes and structures: all those other aspects which go towards the construction of a national cinema.

The series explores and charts a field which is more than ripe for serious excavation. The acknowledged leaders of the field will be reappraised; just as important, though, will be the bringing to light of those who have not so far received any serious attention. They are all part of the very rich texture of British cinema, and it will be the work of this series to give them all their due.

Acknowledgements

Our thanks are due to a number of people who have been helpful in the preparation of this book. We are particularly grateful to Andrew Eaton for a valuable interview outlining the formation and working of Revolution Films, the company responsible for Michael Winterbottom's remarkable output, and we also thank Amy Jackson at the Revolution office for her help. Others who should be thanked include: John Oliver of the Catalogue Department of the British Film Institute; Andrew Spicer, of the University of the West of England, for clarifying Winterbottom's Bristol locations; Judith Armstrong for translating various French passages with more facility than we could have mustered; Kerry O'Hagan for editorial advice; and Monash colleagues, Con Verevis, Melinda Hildebrandt, Adrian Martin and David Sheehy. We are grateful to Accent Film Entertainment and Madman Entertainment, the Australian distributors of, respectively, *9 Songs* and *A Cock and Bull Story*. We also thank Matthew Frost and the team at Manchester for their work in putting this book together. Nearer home, we should like to thank Anna, Maddie and Ella Williams and Geraldine McFarlane for their support and patience.

Introduction

Michael Winterbottom's career in British films should give heart to other aspirants. Without ever having a major commercial success, he has contrived for over a decade to turn out at least one film per year, has shown no sign of slowing down, and has won or been nominated for dozens of awards at festivals from Istanbul to Seattle. He is the most prolific and the most audacious of British filmmakers in the last twenty years. Their names, if not exactly legion, are at least more numerous than for decades: think of Ken Loach, Mike Leigh, Stephen Frears, Shane Meadows, Mike Newell, Pawel Pawlikowski, Richard Jobson, *et al.*, all more than averagely productive, but the *range* of Winterbottom's achievement probably outstrips them all, except perhaps that of Frears. It is not enough of course merely to be prolific. Ralph Thomas was that, with forty-odd titles in thirty years, but the output with one or two exceptions was journeyman stuff. Winterbottom does not merely keep up the pace but never ceases to be innovative and ambitious, on occasion pushing genre conventions out of shape and even extending the frontiers of film. In a recent poll of 'The top 21 British directors of all time', he was placed twelfth and, apart from Shane Meadows, was the youngest on the list.[1] If 'audacious' is a word that leaps to mind in connection with Winterbottom, it should also be applied to anyone writing a book about him: at his production rate, he will be likely to have completed a further two or three films, probably set in daunting locations, as the book is being readied for the printers.

Born in Blackburn, Lancashire, on 29 March 1961, Winterbottom was the son of a teacher mother and a draughtsman father. He attended Blackburn Grammar School and became interested in film following the discovery that the local library ran a film club, introducing him to European directors. He studied English at Oxford University and then spent a year at Bristol University studying film and television. Andrew Eaton, his regular producer, recalled:

We were friends from when we were in our early twenties. When I finished at Cambridge, my best friend at Cambridge went to Bristol University to do a postgraduate film course, and Michael went there when he finished at Oxford, so we both met through this mutual friend. In fact there were four of us who started a company together; it must have been in about 1984.[2]

Both Eaton and Winterbottom had their first experience of film-related work on projects of Lindsay Anderson's. Winterbottom worked with Anderson on a documentary for the BBC about 'saving' the British film industry, really as little more than a 'runner'. Eaton knew Anderson from working at Riverside Studios where 'Lindsay was directing the play, *The Playboy of the Western World* (1984)'.[3] Anderson later helped Eaton to get a job at Goldcrest as a script-reader, and Eaton worked with Anderson on a documentary about John Ford for the BBC (1990). It seems fitting that Anderson should have been an influence in the development of Winterbottom and Eaton; curmudgeonly as he often was, Anderson did have an eye for talent, especially for talent that helped liberate British cinema from what he saw as its too often stultifying, class-based decorums and lack of venturesomeness. He would surely have respected what these two young men, whose early careers he fostered, have achieved.

Winterbottom's television career began in the cutting-rooms at Thames Television, and his first directing experience was on the Thames TV documentaries, *Ingmar Bergman: The Magic Lantern* and *Ingmar Bergman: The Director*, made in 1988 and first screened on ITV and Channel 4 in May 1989. As we shall note elsewhere in this study, Winterbottom's work often seems to be influenced more by European masters than by forebears in British cinema, with the possible exception of Anderson. With producer Alan Horrox, Winterbottom conducted a series of on-screen interviews with some of the great names of Bergman's cinema: cinematographer Sven Nykvist, actors such as Liv Ullmann, Bibi Andersson and Max Von Sydow, scriptgirl and later production manager Katinka Farago, and critic Lasse Bergström.[4] These Bergman films were followed by the Anglo-Hungarian telemovie, *Forget About Me* (1990), which seems not to have been screened in the UK, *Love Lies Bleeding* (1993), a Belfast-set drama centred on the prospect of an IRA cease-fire, and 'The Mad Woman in the Attic', the first episode of the highly regarded series, *Cracker* (1993). What really made his name as a director to watch was the four-part series, the BAFTA-nominated *Family* (1994), the Dublin-set drama of a family of four, each of whom is the focus for one episode.

Of the prentice work in television, little is readily viewable. However, even within the constraints that arise from directing only one episode from a series such as *Cracker*, on which one would assume certain guidelines had been laid down, one can still discern preoccupations that would recur in Winterbottom's later work. In 'The Madwoman' episode, there is the constantly kinetic quality that would mark almost all of his later work. The recurring images are of people on the move, on trains or in cars or striding about streets, and, in this case, particularly of railway tracks, but also of roads cutting a swathe through the landscape or townscape, often with a forward-tracking camera, and there is a song about 'people passing through'. And, indeed, the music will always be crucial to Winterbottom's films, and in this episode there is a haunting series of improvisations on 'Summertime' from *Porgy and Bess*. In the 1995 series of documentaries about early cinema, entitled *Cinema Europe*, produced by Kevin Brownlow and David Gill for their Photoplay Productions, Winterbottom directed the second, 'Art's Promised Land', in which he skilfully blends archival footage with interview material in a tribute to the first great stage of Swedish filmmaking. He had by this time already made the documentaries on Ingmar Bergman, and here he uses interview material with the great Swedish director and others, as he traces the contribution to world cinema of such masters as Victor Sjöström, Mauritz Stiller and Danish Carl Dreyer. From Sjöström, he uses extracts from his poignant and masterly *Ingeborg Holm* (1913), a film which influenced Swedish legislation in regard to the Poor Laws. It is tempting to see in Winterbottom a trace of this kind of socially powerful filmmaking in his chronicle of refugee flight, *In This World* (2003). As well, this *Cinema Europe* episode established Winterbottom as a filmmaker with a sense of tradition, not merely of British but more widely of European filmmaking.

This study of Winterbottom is essentially concerned with his films, and this is fortunate since, as noted, most of his early television work is currently unavailable. However, we shall shortly have an opportunity to view new work for the small screen: at the time of writing, he has just embarked on a series for Channel 4, to be called *7 Days*, which is to be an examination of prison life over five years and the effect on one prisoner's family. Mixing drama and documentary in a way now familiar from some of his film work, Winterbottom's intention is actually to spread the making of the series over five years, to gain a sense of the reality of time passing. As Deborah Allison has written about his earlier television work, 'His years in television engendered some of the most important collaborative relationships that came to dominate his working ethos'.[5] These include screenwriter Frank Cottrell Boyce, who wrote *Forget About Me* and would later write Winterbottom's first feature, *Butterfly Kiss* (1995), and several other ambitious films, including *The Claim* (2001) and *24*

Hour Party People (2002); Trevor Waite, who edited the *Cracker* episode and went on to cut *Family* and all the features up to and including *24 Hour Party People* (2002); Janty Yates, from *Cracker*, who designed costumes for three of his 1990s films (*Jude*, 1996; *Welcome to Sarajevo*, 1997; *With or Without You*, 1999); and actors such as Christopher Eccleston, Kieran O'Brien and Kika Markham, all in the *Cracker* episode, appear in several subsequent features, as do James Nesbitt from *Love Lies Bleeding*, and Des McAleer from *Family*, later in *I Want You* (1998). This practice of surrounding himself with collaborators whom he knew was of course most important in relation to Andrew Eaton, who produced *Family*, and every subsequent Winterbottom-directed film. The practice, which has been reinforced in recent years by the recurrent use of such actors as Steve Coogan and Shirley Henderson, the art director Mark Tildesley and cinematographer Marcel Zyskind, and which is discussed more fully in Chapter 2, may well be an important contributing factor in the prolificacy of Winterbottom's output. There is no doubt a spin-off in efficient working conditions when the director is familiar with what his collaborators can do. As he said, about working with Cottrell Boyce on *The Claim*, in an interview in 2001: 'I think it's always good if you can find someone that you like working with and then it's easier ... And especially with the script, you know? It's a long process working on a script together and I like to be involved in it in terms of feeling like it's going to be a film that I want to make'.[6]

Apart from acting as co-producer on some of his own films (e.g., on *9 Songs* (2004), which he also wrote and edited, and *The Road to Guantánamo* (2006), which he also edited), he has acted as executive producer on several films by other directors. These include: *Resurrection Man* (1998, directed by Marc Evans, whom he knew from his Bristol days); *Heartlands* (2002, directed by Damien O'Donnell); *Bright Young Things* (2003, directed by Stephen Fry), the undervalued adaptation of Evelyn Waugh's *Vile Bodies*; and *Snow Cake* (2006, again directed by Marc Evans). All four of these are produced by Revolution Films, which has by now racked up one of the most impressive filmographies of any company currently operating in the UK. Winterbottom's first big-screen film, *Butterfly Kiss*, was made for Dan Films, British Screen and the Merseyside Film Production Fund; all his subsequent productions have been for Revolution. This has provided a degree of stability and continuity. Eaton has spoken about his working relationship with Winterbottom:

> We never started out with any particular manifesto of what we wanted to do, so we've always been quite flexible. I think it's really good that we're the only directors of the company, and I'm a producer and he's a director

and we don't want to swap places. That seems to work really well. I'd like to think it was some instinct and we made those choices deliberately, but it's sort of worked out well. I think neither of us could have imagined doing films where the decisions about creative and financial matters didn't always go hand in hand. Mike is a really good businessman, and I'd like to think that I have some reasonably good creative ideas, so it seems to me a good marriage.[7]

The 'good marriage' has gone on to produce nearly two-dozen features to the time of writing. In an industry noted for troughs and, indeed, droughts, Winterbottom's production record in this respect is remarkable. It can probably be attributed in varying degrees to the fact that he and Eaton run a lean operation, they draw on regular collaborators, their budgets are very modest by contemporary standards,[8] and they shoot fast. The reporter who commented on interviewing them both at Revolution's office in London was right when she said: 'The company is small and dynamic-feeling, and Winterbottom and Eaton get to make films about the subjects that interest them'.[9] There is sometimes a roughness in the final effect but this also feeds into the over-all sense of immediacy and urgency that underlies such works as *In This World* and *The Road to Guantánamo*. For whatever reasons, Winterbottom has been fantastically busy: is there any other British director of the post-studio years who has made so many films in a little over a decade? And it is not as though these are being briskly filmed in studios in easy reach of London; they are being made all over Europe and elsewhere. His former wife Sabrina Broadbent has written a novel, *Descent* (2004), in which her female protagonist, pregnant and then balancing child and work, struggles to cope with her filmmaker husband's irregular hours and protracted absence. 'You're never here', she accuses.[10] To what extent *Descent* is a *roman-à-clef* is of no consequence here, but without doubt Winterbottom's work schedule has been extraordinary and ubiquitous. Certainly, he has not been one of those filmmakers who spend a lot of time decrying the possibility of making films in Britain.

There is also a refreshing lack of pretension about his approach: he makes films about subjects that matter to him, whether refugees or music or a novel for which he has a passion, but in none of his recorded interviews does one find him engaging in high-toned accounts of what he is up to and he has never associated himself with the *auteur* principle, stressing instead the collaborative aspects of his work.

Where, then, does Winterbottom stand in the history of British cinema and in relation to the contemporary scene? In answer to the first of these questions, there is some sense of lineage. Unsurprisingly, given his early association with Lindsay Anderson, he shows some continuity with the British New Wave. In films such as *Go Now* (1995) and *I Want You*, there is an unaffected interest in working-class lives, though with less sense of 'mission' than we would perhaps associate with those late 1950s/early 1960s directors. With them, in such films as *Saturday Night and Sunday Morning* (1960) and *A Kind of Loving* (1962), one became accustomed to what one critic called 'That Long Shot of Our Town from That Hill',[11] suggesting a level of self-consciousness in the way these films approached their then-novel settings. Winterbottom may echo these films but his use of townscapes is far more unobtrusive: these are just places where people live, not the sites of social statements. As Geraldine Bedell wrote: 'The usual film-making palaver of closing off streets and shutting down restaurants has no appeal for Winterbottom; he likes actors to respond to the places in which they are performing ... In common with Thomas Hardy [whom he has twice adapted], Winterbottom has a profound sense of place, of the environment as both beautiful and benign'.[12] So, though one might at first see his films as descendants of Richardson, Reisz, Schlesinger and Anderson's New Wavers, on closer inspection the differences emerge more clearly: it is with Winterbottom less a response to an overriding middle-classness than a matter of wanting his characters convincingly to belong to, to be shaped by, the places in which the films locate them. Winterbottom claimed, in relation to *Wonderland*, 'I wasn't consciously trying to emulate 60s kitchen sink realism', even if, in the same article, the author, Graham Fuller, argues that 'in the last few years several talented directors have emerged with pain-infused realist dramas that get to the very heart of working- and middle-class Britain'.[13] And Winterbottom has been far more peripatetic in his approach to location-shooting than the New Wavers ever were.

He has more in common with Anderson's restless, emotive *and* cerebral reactions to the worlds in which he situates his films and shares Anderson's absolute eschewal of sentimentality. The dramas of his films are too firmly anchored in reality for access to such facile responses. But just as Winterbottom is probably more honoured elsewhere than in the UK – check out his list of awards and nominations on IMDb – so, too, it is likely that he has been more influenced by such European masters as Bergman and Fassbinder, or the modern iconoclasm of Lars Von Trier, than by his British predecessors. (Such European affiliations are discussed in Chapter 2.) It is hard to detect the influence of specific American filmmakers in his work but there is a very strong sense of generic resonances, as we shall see in Chapter 5. However, by the time he has had his way with, say, the Western, the musical and the road movie as we have become habituated to them in their US incarnations, we may feel that he has turned their conventions inside-out, and that he has subjected them to fresh appraisals.

In post-New Wave Britain, it may be thought that Winterbottom has points of contact with the likes of Ken Loach, Mike Leigh, Shane Meadows and Stephen Frears. And so he does, but in the end his work doesn't *feel* like that of any of the others. He is less overtly and persistently leftist than Loach, though they share a taste for the polemical and for exposing some unattractive underbellies. He shares Leigh's class-based interest in situating his characters in recognisable, scruffy worlds but he is less theatrical than Leigh and lacks the anarchic Swiftian comedy that complicates Leigh's tone. He and Frears have touched on some common stylistic and thematic concerns (think of Frears' sharp account of refugee plights in *Dirty Pretty Things*, 2002), but one can't quite see Winterbottom adapting so smoothly to the narrative habits of classical Hollywood cinema as Frears has on several notable occasions, or to the sentimentality of *Mrs Henderson Presents* ... (2005). Both he and Meadows exhibit a passion for lives lived perilously, and it would be fascinating to see how Winterbottom might address the skinhead ferocities of Meadows' *This Is England* (2007). But he finally seems more wide-ranging than any of these, except maybe (as noted above) than Frears: as Eaton has said of Revolution, it 'doesn't have a set agenda about the type of films we make'.[14] It's not as though he's especially setting out to be 'versatile' or to work his way through the conventional genres, defamiliarising them as he goes; rather one gets the impression of a darting intelligence which is caught by many things going on in the real world, as much as in the world of film or literature. Like all four of those named above, he is concerned for 'the way things are' – and like them he does keep getting his films made. He may not have had a major commercial hit, but he goes on undaunted. He is certainly not one of those British filmmakers derided by director Richard Jobson as being 'like bloody farmers, dependent on subsidies'.[15] He and Eaton may never grow rich, but they have considerably enriched that entity known as British cinema.

Notes

1 *The Telegraph* (14 April 2007), www.telegraph.co.uk/arts (accessed 23 April 2007).
2 Andrew Eaton, interview with Brian McFarlane, London (May 2006).
3 Ibid.
4 In 1988, the British Film Institute published Winterbottom's interviews with Bergman and his collaborators in Paul Gerhardt, Derek Jones and Edward Buscombe (eds), *Working with Ingmar Bergman: Interviews by Michael Winterbottom* (London: British Film Institute, 1988).

5 Deborah Allison, 'Michael Winterbottom', *Senses of Cinema* (May 2005), www.sensesofcinema.com.

6 'IGN', 'Interview with Michael Winterbottom' (9 May 2001), www.filmforce.ign.com/articles/ (accessed 23 November 2004).

7 Andrew Eaton, interview (May 2006).

8 According to IMDb.pro.com, *Welcome to Sarajevo* cost $9m, *Code 46* cost $7.5m, and *In This World* $1.9m.

9 Geraldine Bedell, 'A Winterbottom's Tale', *The Observer* (1 February 2004), www.film.guardian.co.uk/interview/interviewpages (23 November 2004).

10 Sabrina Broadbent, *Descent* (London: Vintage, 2005), p. 105.

11 J. Krish, 'The New Realism and British Films', *Society of Film and Television Arts Journal*, spring (1963), p. 14.

12 Bedell, 'A Winterbottom's Tale'.

13 Graham Fuller, 'A New Generation of Realists Scrap the Kitchen Sink', *New York Times* (23 July 2000).

14 Quoted in Anon., 'Revolution Films', www.skillset.org/film/stories/production/article_3454_1.asp.

15 Quoted in Nemonie Roderick, 'Talking About a Revolution?', *Filmwaves*, 25 (2005), p. 13.

Authorship:
Winterbottom and a body of work

2

As we have already seen, Winterbottom has operated in the social imagination as a British director of formidable note. On the one hand, he has featured in top ten lists in Britain and his name has become a moniker of distinction in the promotion of his own films. He has used a consistent creative team and a stable of actors. On the other hand, his name has become synonymous with an *oeuvre* that skips across genres and styles, often exhibiting connections with a host of filmic influences. In this chapter we attempt to reconcile these disparate positions by, first, articulating the ideas which have led to the name 'Michael Winterbottom' being associated with a particular body of work and, second, by turning to those factors which tend to dissipate the idea of Winterbottom as the single source of a world view and style, and to relocate his films within a constellation of directors, films and (principally European) national cinemas.

A creative team

One traditional way in which one can characterise a director's work, and disperse that same name, is via the notion of a consistent creative team working across a complex *oeuvre*. Of course Winterbottom's long-time collaborative producer Andrew Eaton immediately comes to mind. Winterbottom's professional association with Eaton began as early as their work together on the four-part television series *Family*. Although the two knew each other prior to this, it was Eaton's approach to Winterbottom to direct an adaptation of Roddy Doyle's novel that led to the setting up of Revolution Films. Eaton elucidates:

> So we were kind of friends and our careers were running parallel. He was an editor at Thames for quite a while and when the chance came to do *Family* I had it in my mind that I wanted to work with a director

who was a friend. I just thought it would be a better working experience to work with someone you really knew and trusted. It worked out well. I was lucky because I asked him if he would want to do it and he said yes and then it was his idea to set up the company [Revolution Films]. Just after we finished *Family* he said, 'Why don't we start up a company together with the idea of developing our own scripts?' I don't think we really saw this far down the line but it certainly was the idea of controlling material that we really liked – and ideas that we liked.[1]

Winterbottom brought with him from the first *Cracker* episode editor Trevor Waite who was to edit the next nine Revolution productions including *Family*, *Go Now*, *Butterfly Kiss*, *Wonderland* (1999), *The Claim* and *24 Hour Party People*. Waite was an experienced editor having worked on *Rumpole of the Bailey* (1978–92), *Inspector Morse* (1993) and *Cracker* (1993). On many of these films Waite was assisted by Peter Christelis, who would later edit several films for Winterbottom. Waite also edited several other notable films including Tim Roth's *The War Zone* (1999) and Shane Meadows's *Once Upon a Time in the Midlands* (2002). Frank Cottrell Boyce has been Winterbottom's scriptwriter since the early days. Having cut his teeth on *Brookside* (1987), *Coronation Street* (1991) and the four-part mini series *The Real Eddy English* (1989), Cottrell Boyce first worked with Winterbottom on *Forget about Me*, prior to Revolution Films being set up. This production led to his being brought in by Winterbottom and Eaton to work on *Butterfly Kiss*, *Welcome to Sarajevo*, *The Claim*, *24 Hour Party People*, *Code 46* (2003) and *A Cock and Bull Story* (2006).

Winterbottom has used three principal directors of photography across his features. These are Marcel Zyskind, Alwin Küchler and, for *Wonderland*, Sean Bobbitt. Zyskind began his career in Danish television at the age of eighteen, moving into features as a camera operator for Robby Müller on Lars von Trier's *Dancer in the Dark* (1999) at age twenty. Zyskind first worked with Winterbottom on *24 Hour Party People*, again as camera operator for Robby Müller. His first production as director of photography was on *In This World*, before sharing the role with Alwin Küchler on *Code 46*. This production's multiple locations and hectic shooting schedule combined to require more than one director of photography. For example, to construct the guesthouse sequence late in *Code 46*, Zyskind filmed the exteriors and reception area in India, while Küchler shot Tim Robbins and Samantha Morton in the couple's bedroom in a studio in London.[2] Zyskind went on to shoot *9 Songs*, *A Cock and Bull Story*, *The Road to Guantánamo* and *A Mighty Heart* (2007). Küchler began his career working with Lynne Ramsay on her shorts, *Small Deaths* (1996), *Kill the Day* (1996) and *Gasman* (1997), before moving on to her features, *Ratcatcher* (1999) and *Morvern Callar* (2002), and Kevin Macdonald's *One Day in September* (1999). Küchler was cinematographer on Winterbottom's grander visions, *The Claim* and *Code 46*.

Having started with Revolution Films on the Marc Evans-directed *Resurrection Man*, production designer Mark Tildesley has worked on eleven of Winterbottom's films beginning with *I Want You* right through to *The Road to Guantánamo* and *Murder in Samarkand* (2008). Costume designer Natalie Ward began her association with Winterbottom as wardrobe mistress on *Go Now* and later as costume assistant on *I Want You*. During this period she also worked as assistant on *Elizabeth* (1998) and *Notting Hill* (1999), before beginning work as costume designer on *Wonderland*, *24 Hour Party People* and *Code 46*. Casting director Wendy Brazington first worked with Winterbottom on *Wonderland* and has formed a close association through eight features as well the Revolution Films production of Stephen Fry's *Bright Young Things* and more recently as co-producer (with Andrew Eaton) of *A Cock and Bull Story*.

Although Michael Nyman has composed and performed music for only two Winterbottom films, *Wonderland* and *The Claim*, his music has been used in two others. *9 Songs* reprises Nyman's 'Nadia' and 'Debbie', songs originally included in the soundtrack to *Wonderland*, through having the protagonists, Matt (Keiran O'Brien) and Lisa (Margo Stilley), attend a Nyman concert later in the film. *A Cock and Bull Story* employs Nyman's music for Peter Greenaway's *The Draughtsman's Contract* (1982). Andrew Johnston composed the soundtrack music for *Jude*, *Welcome to Sarajevo*, *I Want You* and *With or Without You*.

Winterbottom has also managed to acquire a stable of actors across his films. These include Shirley Henderson (*Wonderland*, *The Claim*, *24 Hour Party People*, *A Cock and Bull Story*), James Nesbitt (*Love Lies Bleeding*, *Go Now*, *Jude*, *Welcome to Sarajevo*), Steve Coogan (*24 Hour Party People*, *A Cock and Bull Story*, *Murder in Samarkand*), Kieran O'Brien (*Cracker*, *24 Hour Party People*, *9 Songs*, *A Cock and Bull Story*, *The Road to Guantánamo*), John Simm (*Wonderland*, *24 Hour Party People*), Rob Brydon (*24 Hour Party People*, *A Cock and Bull Story*), Christopher Eccleston (*Cracker*, *With or Without You*, *Jude*, *24 Hour Party People*).

General anecdotal approaches to his work consist of remarks about shaky, handheld photography or baffling takes on genres and the periods in which his films are located. This bafflement is encouraged by Winterbottom himself. In a recent interview Winterbottom was asked about 'the apparent absence of *auteurist* fingerprints on his films', to which he responded:

I'm sure it irritates people, but so what? I find that attitude ludicrous because film-making is either an industrial or a collaborative process, whichever way you want to describe it. So to have this bourgeois, liberal-romantic idea of the creator seems to me like the ultimate perversion. All auteur theory has become this: if you make the same film over and over again, and you write your own scripts, you're an auteur; if you don't, you're not. It's so conservative in its approach.[3]

In a survey of the interviews, reviews and articles written about Winter-bottom, one detects an ongoing struggle to link Winterbottom with a particular style or approach to filmmaking; even the notion of an *oeuvre* is seen to be at odds with his eclectic use of genre and different modes of realism. In this chapter we will seek some methods to deal with the notion of authorship in relation to Michael Winterbottom, to under-stand his work better in relation to traditional notions of authorship. In another interview in 2000 Winterbottom was asked, 'which direc-tors have inspired you?' He replied, 'Bergman, Truffaut, Godard, Fass-binder, Herzog, Fellini, Bertolucci, Scorsese, Altman. And in Britain, Carol Reed, Lindsay Anderson, Karel Reisz, Bill Douglas, Nic Roeg, Peter Greenaway, Ken Loach'.[4] This collection of directors suggests some lines of approach to Winterbottom's work.

Some key influences

Ingmar Bergman

Early in his career Winterbottom directed *Ingmar Bergman: The Magic Lantern* for the BBC. The interviews Winterbottom conducted also formed the backbone of the publication, *Working with Ingmar Bergman*, while Peter Cowie contributed introductions to the participants and an essay.[5] The film and book were made to coincide with the release of the Swedish director's autobiography *The Magic Lantern*.[6] Presumably because of his knowledge obtained from the earlier project, producer Kevin Brownlow took on the same team for the 'Art's Promised Land [Sweden]' section of *Cinema Europe*, a six-hour documentary series made for television. Winterbottom directed while Peter Cowie acted as consultant. In the main, 'Art's Promised Land' is concerned with the first 'Golden Age' of Swedish cinema of the 1910s and 1920s including the early directorial careers of Victor Sjöström (later to belong to Berg-man's stable of actors), Mauritz Stiller, and the rise and collapse of the Swedish studio system and production companies. There is a formal connection between Winterbottom's work and Bergman's. In writing about *Butterfly Kiss*, Sinyard and Williams propose;

In its close scrutiny of the relationship between two women and the effect they have on each other, the film seems indebted to *Persona* (1966): the rich religious subtext of the film, with its emphasis on martyrdom and sacrifice, echoes Bergman's recurrent treatment of the same subjects. Eunice howls in the walkway over the motorway about her loss of faith ('God has forgotten me – I kill people and nothing happens'): it reminds us of God's silence in Bergman's *Tystnaden* (*The Silence*, 1962).[7]

As Sinyard and Williams point out, in both films there is a sense of the two women merging into the other.[8] In *Butterfly Kiss* this 'exercise in transference', as Winterbottom has called it, occurs immediately where Eunice (Amanda Plummer) announces, 'Look at us, it's me, here I am', and her abbreviated name, Eu, 'rhymes' with Miriam's (Saskia Reeves) shortened to Mi. But it is *The Silence* that provides a closer formal connection in the form almost of a quotation. Late in *Butterfly Kiss*, after Miriam has killed Mr McDermott (Des McAleer), the women take his car and drive to the beach where Miriam drowns Eunice. Eunice tells Miriam, 'All that time you spent trying to make me good, all you had to do was turn bad yourself'. As Eunice's monologue proceeds, the pair are framed in a medium close-up with Saskia Reeves in profile shot-left while Amanda Plummer addresses us from shot-right. This scene is a mirror image of a scene from *The Silence* where the two sisters Ester (Ingrid Thulin) and Anna (Gunnel Lindblom) are engaged in a conversation after Anna has returned to their apartment with dirt on the back of her dress. Ester confronts her sister regarding her whereabouts, which results in Anna telling her stories of a sexual encounter with a stranger first in a cinema then in a church. *The Silence* is a prelude to the director's later films, in which Bergman's concerns have shifted from theological to psychological.

Krzysztof Kieślowski

I Want You also has connections with European art cinema. Winterbottom employed prolific Polish cinematographer Slawomir Idziak, long-time collaborator of Krzysztof Kieślowski, as director of photography on *I Want You*. This followed the international success of *The Decalogue* (1989–1990), *The Double Life of Veronique* (1991) and *Three Colours: Blue* (1993), all of which featured Idziak's work. Following Kieślowski's films, *I Want You* is an atmospheric genre piece that utilises the kind of imagery found in Kieślowski's films. Idziak uses mirrors and glass to create doubles, bleak landscapes and contrasting close-ups of hands and mouths. The film recalls *Blue* in Idziak's use of blue filters and out-of-focus shots, particularly of figures in the landscape or of pebbles on a beach. As with the interest in sound design and musical motifs found in Kieślowski's films, *I Want You* employs a recurring musical motif, in this case Elvis Costello's titular song, as well as having a budding sound recorder Honda (Luka Petrusic) eavesdropping on Helen (Rachel Weisz) and his sister Smoky (Labina Mitevska from *Welcome to Sarajevo*).

Bill Douglas

One of the more curious members of Winterbottom's list is the Scottish director Bill Douglas. Often understood to be an outsider in British cinema, Douglas fashioned a small yet distinctive career across four feature films. The first three, often referred to as 'The Trilogy', *My Childhood* (1972), *My Ain Folk* (1973) and *My Way Home* (1978), were followed in 1987 by *Comrades*, a film set in Dorset and New South Wales. The Trilogy films were all set and filmed in the town of Newcraighill, close to Edinburgh, a village of miners' cottages in the throes of economic and social collapse. Andrew O'Hagan describes the Trilogy as being concerned with:

> The struggle of a child against the poverty and mental cruelty of a mining village in which opportunities for economic and cultural growth were non-existent and where people seemed proud and pious as a result of their difficulties – resistant to change rather than desirous of it.[9]

John Caughie works to locate the three films, within traditions of Soviet and Northern European cinema providing a connection with Bergman among others:

> Aesthetic distance and intense intimacy, then, is the dialectical tension which marks the trilogy. Bill Douglas seems to me to stand between the formal and visual rhetoric of silent cinema, particularly Soviet silent cinema, and the psychological intensity of the best of European art cinema ... Surrounded by a great deal of blank, marketable international-style quality cinema, both in Europe and in Britain, endlessly recovering a lost past, Douglas's films seem to offer one possibility of an art cinema which is built from the experience of locality, and from difficult and insecure histories.[10]

As we will see further in the next chapter, Winterbottom's films, like Douglas's, rely on a distinct invocation of locality in order to specify the actual, historically located effects of social, political and cultural forces on everyday people.

Nicolas Roeg

Another renegade British director who has fashioned his own particular *oeuvre* outside the parameters usually set for British cinema, as well as developing a set of psychological dramas, is Nicolas Roeg. Like Winterbottom, Roeg has developed a formidable diversity across films such as *Performance* (1970) *Walkabout* (1971), *Don't Look Now* (1973), *The Man Who Fell to Earth* (1976), *Bad Timing* (1980) and *Eureka* (1984). Roeg has displayed the influence of more recent European art cinema in particular that of Alan Resnais, whose emergence from the 'Left Bank' group has led him to be included in the French New Wave.[11] Regarded as one of the most experimental of commercial British directors, Roeg has fashioned a body of work that mobilises time and space, using his trademark flashbacks and particular use of montage techniques. For our purposes, *Eureka* is a valuable companion piece for *The Claim*. Its star, Gene Hackman, in his grizzled frontier-miner persona, provides a considerable model for Peter Mullan's Dillon, and Roeg's film opens with a scene that offers obvious bases for comparison with *The Claim*. Opening with what Salwolke describes as 'an alchemist's dream', images of liquid gold and cosmic figures, the film descends on the Yukon, where we see an overhead shot of two men fighting as a woman tries to intervene outside a hut in a blizzard-swept snowscape.[12] The flashback scene from *The Claim*, in which Daniel Dillon struggles towards an outlying hut in the snow, only to sell Elena (Nastassja Kinski) to Mr Burn (Tom McCamus), seems indebted to this episode in *Eureka*.

Thematically Winterbottom's film recalls Roeg's. Both Dillon and McCann (Hackman) are what are known as 'self-made men', whose lives reached their apotheosis many years before. Both films are concerned with the effects of this 'afterlife' when money can buy anything except their happiness. Both men seek happiness in the places they have built, Dillon in his Kingdom Come (the original title for Winterbottom's film) and MacCann at Eureka, his luxury estate. Whereas in *Eureka* it is a kind of transfer of souls between McCann and his daughter that marks the closure of the film, in *The Claim* it is Lucia (Milla Jovovich) who leaves Kingdom Come after she is replaced by Elena as Dillon's wife, and establishes her own town in the path of the railway line that Donald Dalglish (Wes Bentley) is surveying. In Winterbottom's film, the transfer of souls evident in Roeg's film is rendered as a kind of New World awareness, whereby the commercial opportunity offered by the railway is seized upon by the assertive and wily Lucia, relegating Dillon to the past of the frontier prospectors.

Werner Herzog

In Winterbottom's films the inclusion of references to Werner Herzog's films is another New Wave indicator that forms part of this nexus. In *24 Hour Party People* Ian Curtis is imaged hanging in his flat while the closing scenes from Herzog's *Strozsek* play on the television in the background. This sequence provides a number of points of interest. First, Herzog's film 'rhymes' with Curtis's real life story. Apparently terrified of the impending tour of America that he and his band Joy Division were about to embark on, Curtis committed suicide.[13] In Herzog's film, the main character Strozsek, a German immigrant, is unable to deal with the stultifying nature of American culture, and the film closes with the endless circling of the truck followed by the dance of the chicken on the record turntable. In a sequence reminiscent of the infamous scene in Herzog's *Fitzcarraldo* (1982) where Fitzcarraldo (Klaus Kinski) has the local indigenous Peruvians move a massive steam-ship across a large hillside covered in jungle to reach another river, Winterbottom has Daniel Dillon (Peter Mullan), the owner of Kingdom Come, marry his former mistress Elena (Nastassja Kinski) and decide to move his house to what is presumably a better location.

Another link with the German New Wave is through cinematographer Robby Müller, best known for shooting Wim Wenders' *The Goalkeeper's Fear of the Penalty Kick* (1972), *Alice in the Cities* (1974), *Wrong Movement* (1975) and *Kings of the Road* (1976), all films belonging to the high moment of that country's cinematic resurgence. Müller was approached by Winterbottom to shoot *24 Hour Party People* after he had seen the cinematographer's work on Lars von Trier's *Breaking the Waves* (1996) and *Dancer in the Dark* (2000). By this stage Müller had become a regular cinematographer for Jim Jarmusch, another director with connections to European art cinema similar to Winterbottom's. Müller worked on Jarmusch's *Down by Law* (1986), *Mystery Train* (1989), *Dead Man* (1995) and *Ghost Dog: The Way of the Samurai* (1999).

Robert Altman

As we shall note in chapter 5, it is possible to provide an intertextual relationship between Winterbottom and Robert Altman connecting *The Claim* with *McCabe and Mrs. Miller* (1971). Altman's employment of ensemble casts and fluid camera movement among actors brings together a style that Winterbottom has employed in *A Cock and Bull Story* and *Wonderland*. The Altman work that relates most closely to *A Cock and Bull Story* is *Gosford Park*, partly because of the period setting and the use of a house, in Altman's film the eponymous one and, in *A*

Cock and Bull Story, the mansion in which Tristram Shandy is born and outside of which Captain Toby Shandy (Rob Brydon) plays at war games. Another connection between the two films occurs with Kelly Macdonald appearing as Steve Coogan's partner Jenny in *A Cock and Bull Story* and as Mary Maceachran in *Gosford Park*. The use of McDonald better known for roles in films with contemporary urban settings, films such as *Trainspotting* (1996), *Stella Does Tricks* (1998) and *Splendour* (1999), draws the films closer together. Initially it was Altman's use of Macdonald in his period film that may have surprised some audiences. In Winterbottom's film the surprise is inverted with Macdonald appearing as a contemporary figure in the 'making-of' section of what is largely an historical costume story around which is built the more self-reflexive and comedic elements.[14] This kind of figural intertextuality occurs in the case of Nastassja Kinski's appearance in *The Claim*, which could recall her role as Tess Durbeyfield in Roman Polanski's *Tess* (1979), another Thomas Hardy adaptation antedating *Jude* and *The Claim*. The Altman 'connection' is also to be felt in the fluid interaction of the various relationships which constitute the plot of *Wonderland*: almost inevitably one thinks of how Altman managed such an agenda in *Short Cuts* (1993) and *Nashville* (1975), the latter also seeming to hover over the restless musical ambience of *24 Hour Party People*.

The British New Wave

Winterbottom's own mention of Karel Reisz and Lindsay Anderson provides us with a British lineage that indicates another angle on the term 'new wave'. Winterbottom also began his film career with Lindsay Anderson, describing his job as 'making cups of tea', but this contact with Anderson is likely to have had some influence. One productive way to understand these filmmakers in relation to Winterbottom's work is to recall that their earliest films formed part of what came to be known as the Free Cinema. Starting with a series of programmes at London's National Film Theatre in 1956, Lindsay Anderson's *O Dreamland* (1956), *Wakefield Express* (1956), *Every Day Except Christmas* (1956), Tony Richardson and Karel Reisz's *Momma Don't Allow* (1956), and Reisz's *We Are the Lambeth Boys* (1959), were designed to form a provocation to British cinema. Free Cinema was not, by the accounts of Reisz and Anderson,[15] anything approaching a 'school' of filmmaking, but rather a title arrived at pragmatically as an umbrella for this series of NFT programmes in the later 1950s. Reisz was the NFT's programme director at the time, and the programmes were devised to screen films which were youthful expressions of contemporary filmmakers, whose work was intended to encourage other filmmakers making use of the new portable lightweight 16mm cameras and recording equipment.[16] Like their compatriots in New York City, these filmmakers were making documentaries that embodied the relationship between art and society. Lovell expands:

> This insistence that a direct relationship between the filmmaker and society was valuable seems to have been based on two assumptions: that the portrayal of contemporary society was an essential function of the documentary film, and that art which did not have a direct relationship with society was likely to become trivial and insipid.[17]

Though it is more difficult to see a formal relationship between Winterbottom's *oeuvre* and that of the British New Wave, the notion that film should engage with the contemporary historical world is strikingly apparent in both. In films such as *Welcome to Sarajevo*, *Wonderland*, *24 Hour Party People*, *Code 46*, *In This World*, *9 Songs*, *The Road to Guantánamo* and *A Mighty Heart*, Winterbottom has displayed an engagement with contemporary morality, on both private and public levels.

While Free Cinema has often been understood as a British phenomenon, it is useful to remember here that the Free Cinema programmes also included films by young European directors, connecting the British Free Cinema films with a larger world of American, French and Polish cinema. These films include: *Le Sang des bêtes* (Georges Franju 1956), *On the Bowery* (Lionel Rogosin 1956), *Paragraph Zero* (Walerian Borowczyk 1956), *Two Men and a Wardrobe* (Roman Polanski 1957), *Les Mistons* (François Truffaut 1957), *Le Beau Serge* (Claude Chabrol 1958), and *Once Upon a Time* (Jan Lenica and Walerian Borowczyk 1957).[18] Both Reisz and Anderson went on to make films as part of what came to be understood as the British New Wave with *Saturday Night and Sunday Morning* and *This Sporting Life* (1963) respectively. These were feature films that translated the concerns of the earlier Free Cinema films, such as commentary on contemporary issues, into narrative cinema, again providing models for Winterbottom. As we have seen, Anderson provided mentorship for Winterbottom and Andrew Eaton.

The French New Wave

In his review of *Wonderland*, Bill Mousoulis writes:

> overall, the film is a hotchpotch of various well-known and fashionable elements. There's the British realist vein (Leigh, Loach, *Nil by Mouth*, etc.); the Dogme-like camerawork (though Winterbottom employs a more classical *vérité* form); the narrative and thematic criss-crossings found in films such as *Happiness* (Todd Solondz, 1998); and those ghost-like expressionistic devices such as slow motion, time-lapse and

unnaturalistic [*sic*] sound layerings (seemingly borrowed from Wong Kar-wai). In effect, there is nothing original in this film. But the end result is wonderful, and clearly more than just the enjoyment of the sum of its parts.[19]

Mousoulis's critical approach to Winterbottom's style is adumbrated in another paragraph where he writes:

> One could perhaps speculate that Winterbottom has simply struck it lucky with this film, managing to jell all these elements together in a successful fashion without having to contribute anything original himself to the project. I haven't seen any of his other films, but all I have to do is look at this one to see that he knows what he's doing – 'the evidence is there' (i.e. on the screen), as Jacques Rivette once said about Howard Hawks.[20]

Mousoulis's perceptive approach to Winterbottom and to *auteur* criticism runs against most of the attempts to conceptualise Winterbottom in terms of a consistent style.

Following Mousoulis's invocation of Jacques Rivette and his 'The genius of Howard Hawks' (1953), one may turn to the French New Wave of the 1950s and 1960s, to the criticism of *Cahiers du Cinéma*, and the cinema of Godard, Rivette, Rohmer and others, to connect Winterbottom's *oeuvre* with a particular tradition in world cinema.[21] To further locate Winterbottom in relation to his own list of directors who have inspired him, it may be best to consider what the French New Wave was most concerned with. Jean Douchet, in his *French New Wave*, provides an intuitive account of a film movement in reaction to the classical French cinema and its subsequent new approaches to imaging the street, the body, and, of course, the concept of the *auteur*.[22]

Two 'sites'

The street

In locating Winterbottom's body of films in relation to the work of Jean-Luc Godard and François Truffaut (remembering the inclusion of *Les Mistons* in the Free Cinema programme), consider the manner in which Winterbottom uses locations: in particular, his use of public spaces such as the street. Douchet reminds us how the French New Wave of the late 1950s and 1960s went out into the street, away from studios and 'refused to acknowledge the determinism of the set', to imagine a place where the vibrancy and tragedy of French life abounded.[23] In keeping with a shift away from the 'sophistication' of the French film industry to an engaged, 'amateur' approach to filmmaking, the New Wave film-makers embraced the street.[24]

> The New Wave was interested in the way of life that its young filmmakers had known since 1950. The maid's rooms – so-called student quarters – and even smaller hotel rooms; the minimalist apartments lent or shared with friends; the cafés in the Latin Quarter or near Saint-Germain, pref-erably with a terrace where conversations went on for hours on end. Where books were read, sometimes stolen, or negligently dropped onto a table (providing an opportunity for the viewer to discover the director's favourite authors), where scams for making money or techniques for picking up women were tried out ... The street, as seen by the New Wave, reflected the aspirations of the young people who made it theirs ... Paris was at their feet. It was a place of unlimited possibility.[25]

In films such as *Breathless* (Godard 1960), *The 400 Blows* (Truffaut 1959), *The Sign of Leo* (Eric Rohmer 1962) and *My Life to Live* (Godard 1962), the New Wave provided what Jean Douchet terms 'a more physical confrontation with the outside world'.[26] Like these French New Wave filmmakers, Winterbottom insists, as we will see further in chapter 3, on the use of locations, with considerable emphasis on exteriors where characters engage in conversations crucial to their lives and the life of the film. Many of Winterbottom's films could be understood in relation to that documentary sub-genre: the city film. *With or Without You* (Belfast), *Wonderland* (London), *24 Hour Party People* (Manchester) *Welcome to Sarajevo* (Sarajevo), *Code 46* (Shanghai), *In This World* (Tehran, Istanbul) all seek to divine the ghosts of civilisation at home in the metropolis, the cultural forces that make these places distinct.

While *With or Without You*, *Welcome to Sarajevo*, *Wonderland* and *24 Hour Party People* largely contain their narratives within one metrop-olis, *Code 46* and *In This World* 'come alive' when they set down in the major cities. The sense of wonder experienced by Jamal and Enayatullah upon their arrival in Tehran and later Istanbul is palpable when the pair, respectively, wander the streets eating ice cream in Iran's capital city or play soccer with a soft-drink can on the Bosphorus Bridge. *Code 46* (recalling Godard's use of Paris in *Alphaville: The Strange Case of Lemmy Caution* 1965) uses contemporary Shanghai to imagine a futurist city, a postmodern metropolis with all the contradictions of futurist architec-ture and the traces of old Shanghai in the bars, restaurants and housing in which Maria Gonzalez (Samantha Morton) and her friends live. And as Mousoulis points out, in *Wonderland*, Winterbottom employs slow motion and colour-bleed photography to render the urban world of the characters in a manner recalling, in particular, Wong Kar Waï's *Fallen Angels* (1995).

The body

The representation of bodies in Winterbottom's films has echoes of the French New Wave criticism that emanated from *Cahiers du Cinéma* and resonated out into film criticism worldwide in the ensuing years. With the emergence of a cinema interested in the new modern world, in what Douchet called 'a more physical confrontation with the outside world', came an interest in the human figures that existed in this world, a kind of new body for the modern world, incarnated in such actors as Brigitte Bardot, Jeanne Moreau, Jean-Pierre Léaud, Jean-Paul Belmondo and Jean-Claude Brialy. As Michel Marie points out, much of this new acting style can be traced to the direction of young turks such as Godard, Truffaut, Rohmer and Chabrol, and one effect of their films was an acting style that was at once 'unbalanced, disjointed', particularly in relation to 'nonchalance, ease and cynicism'.[27] With this rise of modern actors and a revolutionary cinema came a critical interest in understanding the phenomenon. This is not to say that Winterbottom belongs to this critical lineage, but that he is possibly the only contemporary commercial director whose work can be understood better with recourse to French New Wave cinema and criticism.

Following from his use of the street, it is possible to understand Winterbottom's approach to imaging the human body as an echo of the French New Wave. As we will see later in relation to notions of filmic realism, Winterbottom's films, because of their emphasis on location, propel characters through the worlds they inhabit. Unlike the realism of a Ken Loach, and the tradition of social-documentary filmmaking, such as that emerging from the Grierson school, Winterbottom uses the body to generate a measure of the times in which it figures. In this manner Winterbottom moves his characters through their world, relying less on dialogue than on documenting their bodily expression in relation to that world. This idea can be seen at work in his road movie, *Butterfly Kiss*, in which Eunice and Miriam are not so much in a physical movement across the landscape as taking a bodily journey involving sex and murder, while surrounded by many of the defining characteristics of the road movie.

Similarly, Michael's moral journey in *Welcome to Sarajevo* is paralleled by the physical journey with the children from the orphanage, and finally with Emira back to London. Visually dominating this journey is Michael's body, which lopes and struggles in ungainly fashion, carrying the weight of the siege of Sarajevo on his shoulders. Stephen Dillane's performance as Michael can be seen as a performance of the body struggling against its environment. Again, Shirley Henderson's performance as Debbie in *Wonderland* is one of battle. Trussed-up and brim-full of aggression, Henderson's body is at once at ease with and in assertion against the pressures of urban life. While Molly (Molly Parker) finds herself at the mercy of the rhythms of London, Debbie rails against her husband, her son and her sisters, marking out her own self-assertion and resistance to the city. Another significant body-type in Winterbottom's films is that of Steve Coogan. In *24 Hour Party People*, Coogan's odd shape (big hips) and angular awkwardness mark the stuffy Cambridge-educated Tony Wilson as ill at ease, with a certain uncomfortableness in his own skin. His foppish long hair, affected accent and, in particular, his way of carrying himself, mean that he stands out in the crowds at the Joy Division gigs he attends. While Wilson claims to have been one of the people behind the Manchester movement, his body, whether being slung around the mosh pits at Siouxsie and the Banshees gigs or agonising over the name of Don Tonay, betrays a comic self-obsession, one literally embodied in Coogan's performance.

Bodies in private and public places: *9 Songs*

Unsurprisingly, the reception of *9 Songs* upon its release focused on the controversy generated by the use of actual sex and its notoriety as 'the most sexually explicit film in UK cinema history passing uncut and granted an 18 certificate by the British Board of Film Classification'.[28] The film was invariably compared with such others as *Intimacy* (2001, UK/France/Germany/Spain), *Anatomy of Hell* (2005, France), *Irréversible* (2002, France), *Baise-Moi* (2000), *Ken Park* (2002, USA) – some for their explicitness, others for their problems with censorship authorities. While comparisons at the level of censorship – the films gained notoriety because of the depiction of actual sex – have generally been rallying points for film communities around the world, this body of films requires a more thorough-going critical approach. It might in fact be more useful to locate *9 Songs* in relation to a number of film and literary texts including Michel Houellebecq's novel, *Platform* (2001), Nagisa Oshima's *In the Realm of the Senses* (1976) and Godard's *Breathless* (1960, France) to examine how the film functions within Winterbottom's *oeuvre*.

In an interview, Winterbottom was asked by Andrew Hennigon 'You've said that Michel Houellebecq's novel *Platform* was an inspiration for *9 Songs*, but did you have any movies as frames of reference?' Winterbottom replied:

> The film wasn't really inspired by *Platform*. One thing that happened before we made *9 Songs* is that we'd asked Michel Houellebecq about the

possibility of making a film of *Platform*. He said that he wanted to direct it, so it wasn't possible. But then we moved on and we thought, OK, let's do a movie about two people making love. One of the starting points of *9 Songs* was: why do films NOT show sex? So many films are love stories, so why not show a love story through two people making love? Why is it that you avoid two people making love when you do a love story? It seems perverse. In that sense, you could say that what inspired me were all the films that avoid sex – including the films that I've made. Before we made this I made a film called *Code 46*, which was a love story, but we kind of skipped over the physical side of the relationship, even though it's two people meeting one night, making love and falling in love. So there was a kind of reaction against those films. I think the only film that was really a starting-point reference for the sex within it was *Ai No Corrida* [1976, directed by Nagisa Oshima], which I saw when I first went to university – the way of getting you to join the film club was by showing you *Ai No Corrida*, because it had lots of sex in it! And it's a great film. It tells the story through sex, but like a lot of films that deal with sex, it deals with sex in quite an extreme form – almost like a metaphor for power and society, and so on. The idea of *9 Songs* was just to use two people making love as a love story; it's simply trying to capture something of the atmosphere of two people being in a love affair.[29]

Winterbottom's own words here provide some indication of a context for *9 Songs*. Houellebecq's *Platform* is a novel replete with explicit pornographic writing. It is his third novel, following *Whatever* [*Extension du domain de la lutte*] (1994) and *Atomised* [*Les Particules élémentaires*] (2000). It focuses on the relationship between Valérie and Michel, two tourists who become involved in a sex-tourist industry resort in Thailand that is immediately successful but leads to Valérie's death at the hands of terrorists and the collapse of the venture. *Platform* weaves a tale of capitalist exploitation, the rise of the tourist industry and its ramifications for local cultures and Muslim extremism. Particularly in its early passages, the novel traces the intricacies of Valérie and Michel's developing relationship through their sexual encounters. It could be said that Houellebecq's novel has only the central sexual relationship between Valérie and Michel in common with *9 Songs*, yet the kind of adaptation that occurs between *Platform* and *9 Songs* also recalls the kinds of literary adaptations or 'pre-texts' of the French New Wave, in particular, Godard's early films. One thinks of the 'adaptations' of *Il Disprezzo* by Alberto Moravia into *Le Mépris* [*Contempt*] (1963), or *Fool's Gold* by Dolores and Bert Hitchens into *Bande à Part* [*The Outsiders*] (1964), or the two short stories 'La Femme de Paul' and 'Le Signe' by Guy de Maupassant into *Masculin Féminin* (1966). In all these films the novels become provocations or preludes to the films derived from them.

As with these adaptations, *Platform* has an initiatory relationship to the finished film, but it is also directly quoted and appears in the film. In one scene Lisa and Matt are both lying on the bed reading in Matt's flat. Lisa's reading from Houellebecq's *Platform* is fragmented, the cover visible in her hands:

> Immediately after undressing, I was a little embarrassed to discover that I had a hard-on, and I lay down on my stomach beside her ... One of them had shaved her pubic hair, you could make out her slender, delicate slit. 'I really go for that type of pussy ...' Valérie said in a low voice. 'It makes you feel like slipping a finger inside' ... As she lay down, you could make out the thick plump lips of her pussy ... I heard footsteps approaching across the sand, I closed my eyes again.[30]

Matt continues to act out the fantasy of *Platform* into the world of *9 Songs*. As he ties Lisa up before covering her in some kind of body oil he says, 'Forget who you are, forget where you are. You're on a beach in Thailand', before performing cunnilingus on her. As Douchet has said, in the films of the French New Wave, these kinds of scenes, with characters reading, enable us to discover the directors' favourite books and to make the kinds of connections we have just done.

As already stated, *9 Songs* alternates between images of real sex and the largely improvised performances of Stilley and O'Brien and then the images and sounds of the concerts. This alternation is less of a dialectic than a disjunction that diminishes the interest in the sexual performances and confers on them a certain banality. Much of this awkwardness stems not from a sense of 'bad' acting but, rather, from the aesthetic that stems from the digital-production, everyday, real setting and location lighting and the relaxed performances of the actors. Both Stilley and O'Brien as actors seem entirely comfortable with their own and each other's bodies. While Winterbottom would have us understand their relationship as a passionate one, in which he wants to focus on the sexual aspects, the very intimate and close-up images of these bodies, in particular Stilley's, are both documented and a matter of performance. The film may or may not be pornography, but it does situate Stilley and O'Brien's bodies in between their acting as their characters and as a document of their bodies in sexual acts. As Jean-Louis Comolli proposes:

> The filmed body is not an imaginary body, even if the fiction refers it to some purely invented character and whatever the phantasies for which it is support. It is not imaginary to the extent that we see its image and know, as soon as we are in the spectator's place, that a real body, the actor's, is required for there to be an image on the body. The body of the imaginary character is the image of the real body of the actor.[31]

This 'doubling' of character and real actors' bodies is a key to 9 Songs. This spectatorial position is emphasised with the documentary effect of digital video and location shooting. The images of Matt and Lisa are, at the same time, those of Kieran and Margot. They seem to be acting themselves, often a criterion of quality, but in this case the two personae aren't sufficiently differentiated to make their relationship interesting. For Winterbottom this poses a problem. To attempt to trace the nuances of a relationship through the sexual encounters, the intimate, domestic renderings of real sex, places pressure on the conversational and attempted 'natural' extra-sexual interactions. Because the sex is so frequent, prolonged and relaxed, the narrative function of the relationship comes across as forced and contrived. The scene where a forlorn Matt watches Lisa masturbate with a dildo is especially mawkish and clumsy.

Ai No Corrida [*In the Realm of the Senses*] is another reference point and one that implicates the Japanese New Wave, of which Oshima was a leading figure. According to Maureen Turin, *In the Realm of the Senses* was proposed by producer Anatole Dauman, a veteran of the French New Wave,[32] to Oshima as a project whereby Oshima could make a hard-core pornographic film without the kinds of restrictions he would encounter in Japan.[33] The other relationship to French culture is hinted at in the way the film's name echoes the title of Roland Barthes's book of essays, *Empire of Signs* (1970), which reverses the relationship, examining Japanese culture.[34]

Oshima's film, like Winterbottom's, is an episodic account of a mutual sexual obsession. In this case between a servant girl Sada Abe (Matsuda Eiko) and her master Kichi-zo (Fuji Tatsuya). Both films feature a different sexual act or performance in each episode. Across Oshima's film the sex acts develop into more extreme sado-masochistic performances as the couple search for the highest states of orgasm. While there is a sense of increasing domination of Sada over Kichi, it is the search for pleasure that motivates the sex acts. *In the Realm of the Senses* also has at its heart the issue of voyeurism: what Stephen Heath calls 'looking at looking'.[35] For Heath, Oshima's film questions the role of the spectator in the apparatus of cinema. While it is clear that we watch the sexual acts performed by Sada and Kichi, it is also the case that we watch these acts as the rest of the characters of the film do. As we have seen, 9 Songs has a documentary quality that elicits a different kind of voyeurism, one that positions the spectator in a 'doubled' relation to the actors' bodies. Heath argues that the notion of desire is introduced in the early scene where Sada watches Kichi make love to his wife. We, as spectators, are asked to see this act as Sada and the other servant does. Immediately our spectatorial position is doubled, and as Heath demonstrates, this look is transferred further from Sada and the accompanying servant to all the other servants who witness the multiple acts. Across the film we see many acts witnessed by many people multiplying the voyeurist possibilities and questioning not only voyeurism but voyeurism as a component of the cinematic apparatus.[36] So the 'doubling' that occurs in 9 *Songs* is an effect of characters and their bodies being split at the level of spectatorship. In *In the Realm of the Senses* the kind of voyeurism generated is a result of the spectator herself being doubled.

Like Oshima's film, 9 *Songs* attempts to displace the voyeuristic potential of pornography through presenting the film as a vision of Matt's (Kieran O'Brien) recollections. The opening of the film sets this up. The pre-title sequence commences with the silent image of a bright-red plane flying over snowfields. As the shot holds, the hum of its engine is faded in to the image. Another shot of the plane follows and the third introduces a man's profile complete with coat, sunglasses and cap. His voice-over begins, later interspersed throughout the film. 'When I remember Lisa, I don't think about her clothes or her work, where she was from or even what she said'. This line accompanies an image of the plane's shadow across the snow and ice. The next image is of a woman's face flitting in and out of the darkness as a shoulder darkens and then moves to release her face into light. The voice-over continues; 'I think about her smell, her taste, her skin touching mine'. The next shot is of the neon exterior of the Carling Brixton Academy Theatre announcing the appearance of Black Rebel Motorcycle Club. Next voice-over: 'The first time I met her was at the Brixton Academy'. This pre-title sequence establishes the perspective of this man whose voice-over we hear. We are also told, in effect, that there is going to be little about the details and history of the people in this relationship, just a remembrance of a physical relationship from a masculine point of view. But it also proves to be a remembrance interspersed with the documentary footage of rock music performances attended by the protagonists. In this way the film is a kind of docu-drama in the manner of Winterbottom's next film, *The Road to Guantánamo*. The performance of the sex acts is juxtaposed to the rock music performances at the Brixton Academy. The intimate domestic sex acts in close-up contrast with the collectivity of the rock performances. While Matt and Lisa are imaged among the crowd at the concerts, they are just a part of a larger event. In the intervening episodes, Matt and Lisa are alone together in Matt's flat. At the Brixton Academy they are part of a massive seething crowd of patrons, part of a communal performance. We are asked to understand the relationship between these public and private performances. Kieran O'Brien's and, in particular, Margot Stilley's awkward improvisation in the flat contrasts with the volume and staging of a rock crowd. There is a vitality and dynamism to the images and sounds at the Brixton Academy that contrasts with the stillness and starkness of the scenes at Matt's flat.

The relationship between the private and public realms is made more explicit with the inclusion of the scene when Matt and Lisa visit the Venus lap-dancing club. Lisa mostly watches the dancer while Matt watches Lisa's enjoyment of the act. As the scene proceeds, Lisa's masturbation is interspersed with the dancer's act. This amalgam of the two performances, as Matt remembers them, says more about Matt's paranoia and the increasing dissatisfaction with their sexual encounters than any sense of moral privilege. Whereas Sada and Kichi, in *In the Realm of the Senses*, search for the ultimate orgasm, Matt and Lisa struggle to maintain the sexual heights of their early encounters. As the sexual encounters diminish in intensity, Lisa searches for satisfaction on her own and Matt feels isolated. Yet it is Lisa who terminates the relationship by returning to America.

In keeping with the scope of each film, *In the Realm of the Senses* culminates in death, a superior climax, while in *9 Songs* Matt and Lisa split, with Matt exiled to the isolation of the Antarctic. In all the film's 'realms', his flat, the Brixton Academy, the Venus club, Matt seems to be uncomfortably alone. Even the intimacy of his relationship with Lisa is compared to the Antarctic: 'Claustrophobia and agoraphobia in the same place, like two people in a bed'.

Another approach to *9 Songs* might consider the figures of Kieran O'Brien and Margot Stilley in relation to a hallmark of the French New Wave: Kieran O'Brien looks not unlike Jean-Paul Belmondo in Godard's *Breathless*, though without Belmondo's level of affectation, while the unknown Margot Stilley recalls the American Jean Seberg. As in Godard's film, much of the action occurs in an apartment replete with improvised acting, handheld cameras and natural light. Late in *9 Songs*, after Lisa has told Matt that she in returning to the US, she says that he looks like a gangster, again recalling Belmondo's Michel Poiccard. This commingling and distilling of *Platform*, *In the Realm of the Senses* and *Breathless* suggests a provocative intertextuality for *9 Songs*, embracing both the French and the Japanese New Waves. But despite *9 Songs*' acting as a kind of nexus for a list of intertexts, it also represents Winterbottom's most assertive *auteurist* moves. The already mentioned use of *Platform* and the inclusion of footage of his favourite composer Michael Nyman's 60th birthday concert as part of the narrative-fiction component of the film exemplify this assertion. The use of Nyman's songs, 'Debbie' and 'Nadia', in both the fictional world of 9 Songs and as a document of the concert, again elides the easy distinction between these modes of cinema.

It is possible to locate in Winterbottom's *oeuvre* a host of intertextual links to films, directors, actors and film schools, and it is fascinating and rewarding to locate his body of work within a larger constellation. In his schooling in, and gleaning from, movements such as the French, German and Japanese New Waves, it may be most instructive to situate Winterbottom outside of traditional notions of national cinema and explore his work in relation to the panoply of post-New Wave European directors. Like Ken Loach with his *Fatherland* (1986), *Land and Freedom* (1995), *Carla's Song* (1996) and *Bread and Roses* (2000), Winterbottom has taken his filmmaking to other locations and contexts and adapted styles to complement the telling of those stories.

Notes

1 Andrew Eaton, interview (May 2006).
2 Bob Davis, 'A World Apart', *American Cinematographer*, 85: 9 (September 2004), p. 60.
3 Winterbottom quoted in 'British Directors: Open Mike', *Sight & Sound*, 10 (October 2004), p. 31.
4 Michael Winterbottom in *Wonderland* Production Notes.
5 Paul Gerhardt, Derek Jones and Edward Buscombe (eds), *Working with Ingmar Bergman*.
6 Ingmar Bergman, *Magic Lantern: An Autobiography*, trans. Joan Tate (London: Hamish Hamilton, New York: Viking Penguin, 1988).
7 Neil Sinyard and Melanie Williams, 'Living in a World That Did Not Want Them: Michael Winterbottom and the Unpopular British Cinema', *Journal of Popular British Cinema*, 5 (2002), p. 117.
8 *Ibid.*, p. 117.
9 Andrew O'Hagan, 'Homing' in Eddie Dick, Andrew Noble and Duncan Petrie (eds), *Bill Douglas: A Lanternist's Account* (London: BFI, 1993), p. 209.
10 John Caughie, 'Don't Mourn – Analyse: Reviewing the Trilogy' in Dick, Noble and Petrie (eds), *Bill Douglas: A Lanternist's Account*, p. 202.
11 Scott Salwolke, *Nicolas Roeg: Film by Film* (Jefferson, Nth. Carolina and London: McFarland and Co., 1993), p. vii.
12 *Ibid.*, p. 93.
13 At the time of writing Joy Division music video director and band photographer Anton Corbijn's film *Control*, based on Deborah Curtis's book *Touching from a Distance* (London: Faber and Faber, 1996), has just been released.
14 A similar inversion occurred with the use of Gillian Anderson's appearances as Lily Bart in Terence Davies's *The House of Mirth* (2000) and as the Widow Wadman in *A Cock and Bull Story*, when she had been known for her contemporary roles.
15 See interviews in Brian McFarlane (ed.), *An Autobiography of British Cinema*

(London: Methuen/British Film Institute, 1997), pp. 11–12, 476–7.

16 Alan Lovell, 'Free Cinema' in Alan Lovell and Jim Hillier (eds), *Studies in Documentary Film* (London: Secker and Warburg/British Film Institute, 1972), pp. 135–6.

17 *Ibid.*, pp. 136–7.

18 *Ibid.*, pp. 160–7.

19 Bill Mousoulis, 'The Unbearable Lightness of Being: *Wonderland*', *Senses of Cinema*, 7 (2000), www.sensesofcinema.com/contents/00/7/wonderland.html.

20 *Ibid.*

21 More recently it is possible to see a connection with the French New Wave through Winterbottom's use of Kika Markham and Jeanne Balibar. Markham, who initially worked with Winterbottom on 'The Madwoman in the Attic', his episode of *Cracker*, and later in *Wonderland*, appeared in François Truffaut's *Les Deux Anglaises et le Continent* (1976) and Jacques Rivette's *Noroît* (1976) while Balibar, who appeared in *Code 46*, acted in Rivette's *Va Savoir* (2001) and *Ne Touchez pas la hache* [Do Not Touch the Axe] (2007) and Olivier Assayas's *Late August, Early September* (1998), *Clean* (2004) and *Noise* (2006).

22 Jean Douchet, *French New Wave*, in collaboration with Cédric Anger, trans. Robert Bonnono (New York: D.A.P./Distributed Art Publishers, Inc. in association with Éditions Hazan/Cinémathèque Française, 1998).

23 *Ibid.*, p. 122.

24 Douchet's book rewrites his earlier article 'La Rue et le studio [The Street and the Studio]', *Cahiers du Cinéma* (May 1989), pp. 419–20.

25 Douchet, *French New Wave*, pp. 123, 126.

26 *Ibid.*, p. 127.

27 Michel Marie, *The French New Wave: An Artistic School*, trans. R. Neupert (Malden MA and Oxford: Blackwell, 2003), pp. 116–17.

28 *The Guardian*, 19 October 2004.

29 Adrian Hennigon, 'Michael Winterbottom Interviewed', *BBC Movies* (3 March 2005), www.bbc.co.uk/films/2005/03/03/michael_winterbottom_9_songs_interview.shtml.

30 Michel Houllebecq, *Platform* [2001] (London: Vintage Books, 2003), pp. 312–14.

31 Jean-Louis Comolli, 'Historical Fiction: A Body Too Much', *Screen*, 19: 2 (Summer 1978), p. 42.

32 Dauman produced such films as Alan Resnais's *Nuit et brouillard* [*Night and Fog*] (1955), *Hiroshima Mon Amour* (1959) and *Muriel: or the Time of Return* (1963), Chris Marker's *Letter to Siberia* (1957) and *La Jetée* (1962), Jean Rouch and Edgar Morin's *Chronicle of a Summer* (1961) and Jean-Luc Godard's *Masculin Féminin* (1966) and *Two or Three Things I Know About Her* (1967).

33 Maureen Turim, *The Films of Oshima Nagisa: Images of a Japanese Iconoclast* (Berkeley, Los Angeles, London: University of California Press, 1998), pp. 125–6.

34 *Ibid.*, p. 126.

35 Stephen Heath, 'The Question Oshima' in *Questions of Cinema* (London: Macmillan, 1981), p. 149.

36 *Ibid.*, p. 149.

The realist

3

It is tempting to begin writing on realism in Michael Winterbottom's *oeuvre* by considering it in relation to realist traditions in British cinema. As we have just seen, any close consideration inevitably draws attention away from the lineage that includes Ken Loach, Mike Leigh, Shane Meadows and the canonical directors of British cinema, out into the wider and more varied realm of European filmmaking, in particular the New Waves of France and Germany in the 1960s and 1970s. It is important to acknowledge that all of his films employ realism across a variety of styles, genres and historical representations. In this chapter we will focus on *Welcome to Sarajevo*, *Wonderland*, *In This World* and *The Road to Guantánamo*, with a brief reference to *24 Hour Party People* (discussed at greater length in chapter 5) as five very different films that have particular relationships with the historical world that they represent. Each of these films adopts the stylistic attributes most appropriate to the stories being told and to the historical world in which they are set.

Winterbottom's concern for realism, for the most *appropriate* form of realism for the story he tells, can be traced back to the filmmaking that emerged from the French New Wave, originating with a tributary that ran from Roberto Rossellini and Jean Rouch into the early work of Eric Rohmer, Jacques Rivette, Jean-Luc Godard and François Truffaut. In this regard one notes Winterbottom's love of images from location-shooting, of improvised acting and types rather than fully-fledged characters, and a concern with historical context and contemporaneity. Generally, Winterbottom renders his filmic worlds 'in motion'. Characters move incessantly, discussing even the most serious of matters while walking or driving. Cameras move just as much, tracking these characters within the worlds they inhabit, immersed in a mise-en-scène that envelops them and, at the same time, gives rise to their stories.

Winterbottom's films have been characterised by recent critics as having shaky, handheld camera movement and kinetic editing rhythms, and this is certainly true of films such as *In This World, Welcome to Sarajevo* and *24 Hour Party People*. However, a closer inspection of his films reveals a marked consistency, despite the perceived variation in genres and themes, a consistency that derives from a basic realist mode that closely attends to the historical import of the drama at the heart of all his films.

The figure of Rossellini provides a useful way into thinking about Winterbottom's work in relation to the historical imperative that motivates these films. Rossellini's earliest films *Rome, Open City* (1945) and *Paisà* (1946) provide a useful comparison with *In This World* and *Welcome to Sarajevo* in particular.

In This World

In This World employs a voice-over (by Paul Popplewell) and maps which track the journey of Jamal and Enayatullah and which recall the same techniques in *Paisà*. Possibly the most melodramatic scenes in *In This World* occur when the container holding Jamal, Enayatullah and their fellow refugees arrives at Marseille. After the truck is unloaded, and Jamal and Mehti are found to be the only ones alive, Jamal sprints from the loading-dock out on to the streets of Marseille. As he turns out of the dock on to the road, the camera retreats and the frame takes in more of the surrounding world. This scene recalls a similar one from *Rome, Open City*: later in Rossellini's drama, the apartment block central to the film is being searched by the Germans and some of the men, suspected of being members of the Resistance, are detained to be transported for interrogation. As the camera pulls away from the crowd outside the apartment block, Pina (Anna Magnani) runs toward the truck and the camera, screaming for her husband Francesco (Franceso Grandjacquet), imprisoned on the truck. As the camera continues to move, Pina is gunned down as her figure recedes in the frame. This is the high moment of melodrama in Rossellini's film. These formal comparisons, although slight, can be further generalised by pointing to how Rossellini's film, with its ragbag of film stocks, inconsistent lighting and mixture of cinematic modes (observational documentary, newsreel, melodrama), can be compared with *In This World*, which is also often unclear, clumsily lit, using non-actors, an episodic structure and elliptical narrative.

Like *Rome, Open City* or *Paisà, In This World* is a filmmaker's response to real-life contemporary historical events. It grew out of an interest on the part of the director and the screenwriter, Tony Grisoni, in an area of the world which has become a locus for issues of immigration and people-smuggling in the post-9/11 era. Again, as if Winterbottom were following a neo-realist model, these issues directly impacted on the whole production in its research, production and reception. However, as Winterbottom says, the idea for the film came from a general interest in the manner in which immigration was harnessed: 'It was more to do with the last election [June 2001] and how refugees and immigration became an issue for all parties – their thing was to say that they were going to send them all back, and make the conditions here as horrible as possible'.[1] This issue was emphasised by the images of the tragedy in June 2000, when fifty-eight Chinese immigrants died from asphyxiation while being smuggled to London in a lorry. And the 9/11 attacks directed the focus for these issues to the Middle East, in particular to Afghanistan.

Winterbottom and Grisoni travelled to Pakistan in November 2001 to scout for locations and for situations that could inform what turned out to be a largely improvised narrative. They visited the Shamshatoo refugee camp in Pakistan where the film opens. Even the 'casting' of the main characters grew out of the chaotic nature of the locations. Wendy Brazington, Winterbottom's regular casting director, flew to Pakistan armed with the idea of a massive open-air casting session and a list of contacts that Winterbottom and Grisoni had obtained on their earlier trip. Brazington was advised against the casting session, so she had to turn her attention instead to finding the numerous English-language schools scattered throughout the cities. Eventually this led to the discovery of Jamal, while they happened upon Enayatullah at an Afghan market in Peshawar, where he worked in his family's TV and Hi-Fi shop.[2]

The structure of *In This World*, or what Grisoni calls 'the spine', inhered in how the narrative was understood by Winterbottom and his scriptwriter. This spine derived from such questions as 'where you go from, and to, how do you get there, which borders do you have to cross, and how do you cross over those borders. That's what we've got instead of a narrative'.[3] This meant that the processes of immigration and people-smuggling, including the severe practicalities of negotiating violent and life-threatening situations, developed into the narrative. This notion recalls what Jean Douchet says about Rossellini: that in his cinema 'we return to film's origins, to the Lumière brothers, that is, back to current events and journalism when the dramatic force of real events was sufficient to drive a story forward'.[4]

As suggested above, *In This World* is a road movie, and the film also emphasises the danger, tedium, and the enormity of the distances travelled by the refugees Jamal and Enayatullah. Shot in Pakistan, Iran,

Turkey, Italy, France and England, the film's narrative is intimately involved with its locations. This narrative is a rendering of the journey that would be, and is, taken by its protagonists Jamal and Enayatullah to travel illegally from Pakistan to England. As Grisoni recalls, the moment in the film when Jamal and Enayatullah are escorted from the bus on the suspicion of being Afghani had a real-life incident as a precursor. While Grisoni and Winterbottom were on their research trip they were stopped at a road-block and came under immediate suspicion because of the camera and other equipment in their possession. The pair was made to wait for a long time while the soldiers called ahead to obtain verification of their permission to travel. One of the soldiers asked to borrow Grisoni's cheap biro pen and took a liking to it. Owing to the pressure of the situation, exacerbated by the length of time they had been detained, Grisoni became indignant and demanded his pen back, escalating the tension. Because they were about to be released, Winterbottom, who had witnessed the scene between the two men, told Grisoni, 'Toni, let him have the fucking pen!'[5] This incident is mirrored in the scene where Jamal offers the soldier Enayatullah's walkman to ease the situation the protagonists find themselves in and to enable their release. The economic, political and cultural tensions apparent in these Middle Eastern countries are seen in microcosm in these intricate minor incidents, which are, in turn, born of the places in which they happen. These circumstances also recall Rouch's experiments with narrative in films such as *Moi, Un Noir* (1958) and the New Wave predilection for the 'plan-of-action' script. This method, outlined by Francis Vanoye, can be distinguished from the so-called 'programme script' of classical cinema where a 'script organises the story into a fixed structure', compared with which the '"plan-of action script" is more open to the uncertainties of the production, to chance encounters and ideas that come to the auteur in the here-and-now of filming'.[6]

Crucial to this lineage of neo-realism as it runs into the French New Wave and informs this discussion of *In This World* is the use of non-actors or performers whose particular style is based on physicality rather than on the psychological acting of classical cinema. One of the myths that surrounds the neo-realist films is that the Italians in the post-World War II era used real people to play the roles and that is one reason for its particular documentary-like quality. Rossellini denies this. He says:

> Too many believe that the secret of neo-realism rests in having an unemployed man play the role of an unemployed man. I select my performers on the basis of their physical appearance. You can pick up anybody in the street. I prefer non-professionals because they do not have preconceived ideas. I watch a man in his day-to-day life and get him embedded

in my memory. Facing the camera, he will no longer be himself. He will be confused and try to act; which has to be avoided at any cost. A non-professional always repeats the same gestures, his muscles work like that. In front of the camera, he is as though he were paralysed. He forgets who he is, thinking that he was chosen for the role because he has become an exceptional human being. I have to bring him back to his real nature, to reconstruct him, to teach him again his usual gestures.[7]

As mentioned above Jamal and Enayatullah are both actors who emerged from the real world that the film seeks to represent. In this way they are what John Grierson called 'social actors', people who embody the world they belong to. *In This World* is probably Winterbottom's most physical film, based on a journey by individuals, often on foot, and its protagonists personify this physicality. Jamal and Enayatullah, who have little in the way of dialogue, each have a distinctiveness deriving from their dissimilar figures. Jamal is stocky and cheeky, is always telling jokes and laughing, while Enayatullah is lean and tall with an engaging smile and a certain composure. While their journey is elliptical and episodic, their differing personalities emerge as they are carried along by the immense difficulties and complications of their flight out of the Middle East.

Welcome to Sarajevo

Welcome to Sarajevo invites comparison with the Florence episode of *Paisà*. Both films are stories of a city under siege. Based on Michael Nicholson's book *Natasha's Story*, Winterbottom's film was made in the months following the end of the siege of Sarajevo. The film has a strong sense of location with shooting occurring among the rubble-covered streets, burned-out buildings, and the desolation of an immediate post-war landscape. Like Rossellini's film, *Welcome to Sarajevo* is concerned with how the conditions of the city under siege impact on the people of the city, such as Risto Bavic (Croatian actor Goran Višnjić) and his friends, and the orphaned Emira (Emira Nusević). As in Rossellini's early films, there is a mixture of newsreel, drama and documentary. *Welcome to Sarajevo* opens with black-and-white video footage taken from a moving vehicle as it wends its way along a road hemmed by destroyed buildings. As the scene progresses, the images turn to colour and Winterbottom employs more colour television news footage of what may be described as pre-war Sarajevo, home of the 1984 Winter Olympics and the cultural centre of the Balkans, including the markets, parks and young people, as if to illustrate the 'young lovers' of Van Morrison's song that is featured here. As in *The Road to Guantánamo*, Winterbottom melds television news footage of the siege, of massacres and snipers, with the fictional footage taken by his protagonists, Michael Henderson (Stephen Dillane) and cameraman Gregg (James Nesbitt). Like Rossellini's episodic, elliptical *Paisà*, *Welcome to Sarajevo* employs set-pieces or encounters to form a loose narrative pattern. For example, the first half of the film principally involves Henderson, Gregg and the other journalists holed up in the Sarajevo Holiday Inn, scouting for stories to send back to their television stations for broadcast. As word of events, such as a bombing, reaches the hotel, the crews dash to the scene by car to take footage from which to fashion a story. In one of these episodes, the crews are called to a market massacre: as they enter the marketplace, the film freezes on an image of the newsmen faced with the horror of the massacre, before we witness the real-life documentary footage familiar to many people around the world, including the graphic image of the near-severed foot of a woman as she is carried from the scene. Winterbottom stresses the way this footage and that taken by Gregg merge, asserting the efficacy of his own fiction and its responsibility in relation to the historical events of Sarajevo in 1992–1996.

Welcome to Sarajevo employs the character of Michael Henderson to provide an inquiring and moral perspective on the historical events going on around him. Michael is a journalist caught between reporting the sensational events, like those Flynn (Woody Harrelson) thrives on, and the events that he sees as germane to the conflict in the Balkans, such as the plight of the children in the orphanage. We get to know Michael through the historical events that shape his responses. It is through the interaction of the physical world of a besieged Sarajevo and his task of rendering that experience in sound (he does the voice-overs for his reports) and image, directed by himself and shot by Gregg, that we come to know as much as we do about Michael. His actions yield what we know of his character.

At the opening of the film he is clearly frustrated with his role as a news reporter. Responding to Gregg's estimation of Flynn's actions in removing the bride's mother from the street after she is shot – 'I suppose he was only trying to help' – Michael asserts, 'We're not here to help, we're here to report'. This statement is not just an articulation of his frustration with his own inability to have some effect on the war; it is also an expression of his view of the importance of his work as a journalist. Later in the film he is forced into a practical role rather than the reactive journalist's function he is used to. When his efforts to represent the plight of the orphanage are stymied by the news networks and the United Nations, and by the discovery of Milosevic's internment

camps for Muslims, he decides to travel with Emira and to take her back
to England. For him, the inability to have an effect in Sarajevo creates a
moral dilemma.

Michael, like most of Winterbottom's characters, is presented in very
physical terms: he is incessantly walking, running, driving, entering
rooms or leaving them. He is direct and succinct, with a clipped English
accent. He is not one for extemporising or expressing himself in any
way other than with brief assertive words. He is not satisfied with his
own role as a reactive reporter of events in Sarajevo. It is not until he
locates the cause of the orphanage and the singular project of Emira, to
whom he promises safe passage out of Sarajevo, that he seems moti-
vated by a moral cause.

Welcome to Sarajevo is possibly Winterbottom's most uneven film.
This is not to say that it is of lesser quality than the others, but that it has
a dynamism and fidelity to the events it depicts which means that the
film lurches from one scene to the next, struggling to give coherence to
events that are almost inexplicable in any formal sense. In keeping with
the physicality of Michael and the other journalists who race around
Sarajevo either dodging snipers' bullets or sprinting to beat the next
person to the news story, *Welcome to Sarajevo* has a visceral quality
further effected by its combination of video, 35mm, Super 8 and broadcast news footage. As Michael Atkinson writes:

> Outrage is cheap and Winterbottom prioritises instead the visual environ-
> ment he dumps us into, making sure the action cascades across the rest-
> less frame (and beyond) without signs of jerry-rigging, dramatic setups/
> rewards, emphatic emotional engineering, or cheap structural ideas like
> redemption or 'character arc'. The film's primary story, of Henderson
> deciding to smuggle a young orphan girl out of Bosnia and bring her
> home to England with him, arises out of the Ernstlike rubble with no
> forewarning – it's just something merciful that happened, naturally and
> humanely, somewhere in the funhouse urban horror of the un-designated
> 14th worst place on earth.[8]

Atkinson's words convey the way in which Winterbottom depicts the
ruins of Sarajevo as they give rise to the stories of Michael, Emira,
Risto and the others. Not only is Sarajevo in ruins but also the resulting
stories, as in Rossellini's film, are fragmented, partial and incomplete.
Emira has been smuggled to London but we have no sense of how she
will fare; similarly, the doorman (and later 'gangster'), Zelkjo (Dražen
Šivak), emerges as a man of influence in Sarajevo, yet his story diminishes in the film once Emira's mother, Munira Hodzic (Vesna Orel), has
been located and Emira's adoption papers are signed. It is the pressure
of the war that has fractured these narratives and these people.

Through its mixed modes, dynamic editing, fractured narratives and visceral, physical movement, Winterbottom's film renders a confusing, incomplete set of narratives which convey the effect of a civil war on the journalists attempting to represent these events as well as the everyday inhabitants of Sarajevo. In this way, while not his best-known film, *Welcome to Sarajevo* marks a point of emergence of a more considered and historically contingent realist mode that would be adapted to the narratives and locations of Winterbottom's next films.

Wonderland

Wonderland is another film that invokes a strong sense of place from which to conjure a story. As mentioned above, *Wonderland* draws its imagery from the location-shooting of London streets, bars and public life. Winterbottom has spoken about the emphasis on location in the film:

> The film is set in very specific parts of London – a section of south London between Vauxhall, Elephant and Castle and Brixton, and Soho. And because of the way we decided to film, we shot everything in what we felt was the 'real' location. For example, in the script, Nadia worked in a café in Soho. Now, often when you make a film you might want to shoot that café scene somewhere else, just to make it easier. But on *Wonderland* we always shot in the real place – so her café is in Old Compton street. What is more, because we shot on real locations, without extras, and when they were open, we had to shoot at the same time as the events were happening. For example, the opening scene of the film takes place in the Pitcher and Piano bar in Soho. Normally a film would take over a location like that, close it down, fill it with extras, and probably shoot a nighttime scene at 10 o'clock in the morning. For us to get that 'end of the night' scene we had to wait there *till* the end of the night, wait until everyone was drunk and getting ready to go home, before we could get the right atmosphere. So the film is incredibly specific in its setting.[9]

Following this specificity of locations, *Wonderland* uses them to fashion a sense of immediacy for the characters, who are all at the mercy not only of the events in their lives but also of the hurly-burly of urban living in London. The most obvious example of this is the sequence in which Jack (Peter Marfleet) goes to the Guy Fawkes celebrations. Jack is like a cork in the ocean, buffeted and bobbing among the crowd until he is literally knocked down, attacked and robbed by several boys. Some of the most potent scenes in *Wonderland* are the crowd scenes at the football match where Jack sits alone, whether with his father Dan (Ian Hart), or by himself when Dan lights out for a beer. The film's signature scenes are marked by the blurred-motion images of the film's characters on the move, whether it is Nadia (Gina McKee) fleeing her lonely hearts date, or Eddie (John Simm) cruising the streets on his scooter looking for the reason why he left his job, or the poignant image of a weeping Nadia on the rowdy bus home on a rain-drenched night after the date with Tim (Stuart Townsend). All these scenes employ images where the lone characters are located among the hurly-burly of the urban environment.

In contrast to the fleeting urban images of *Wonderland* are the domestic scenes of intimacy between characters, such as when Debbie (Shirley Henderson) takes her lover back to the hairdresser's for sex, or when Bill (Jack Shepherd) locks himself out of his flat and stops over at Donna's (Ellen Thomas), where he drinks a cocktail and dances, relaxing and enjoying himself away from the misery of a loveless marriage. The most poignant of these scenes occurs when Eileen (Kika Markham) attends the bingo hall in what seems to be a regular respite from her domestic hell. Markham's forlorn persona draws on a long history of British working-class typage in cinema, particularly in the films of the British New Wave (think of Rachel Roberts in *This Sporting Life*, 1963). This scene is a sophisticated representation of a traditional public space that provides a haven from both public and domestic life, where working-class women can remain by themselves in a dispersed crowd interconnected by the game of bingo and the public institution of feminised gambling. Winterbottom renders this world in a terse montage of individual shots overlain with the melancholy of Michael Nyman's minimalist score. The effect here is that, within the scene, there is a shift from character type and narrative to a documentary tone, taking the lives of the particular characters of *Wonderland*, such as Eileen and Bill, out into the wider public realm of working-class London away from the trendy bars and coffee shops of Soho.

In one of the early scenes in *Wonderland*, Nadia is imaged in a public bathroom (actually shot in the Pitcher and Piano bar in Soho). We can hear some muffled crowd noises in the background. The camera frames her to the right looking into a mirror. As she prepares herself for a meeting, Nadia opens the door and emerges into the crowded bar. The camera follows her as she worms her way through the crowd to find her friend, Alex (Nathan Constance). This is a telling introduction to the character of Nadia, the café worker seeking companionship through a lonely hearts club. In this scene Nadia steels herself for her engagement with Alex, but also against the crowd of pub patrons. Physically, Nadia is self-contained and introverted, shoulders hunched in defence against the world. These aspects of her character are accentuated in the following scenes where Nadia flees the meeting with Alex to walk the streets of London's Soho district with her hair tied tightly, her back-pack in place, her shoulders hunched, her hands tucked into her pockets and arms into her sides. In this district of London, bars crammed with twenty-somethings on the make, Nadia is alone, trussed up against the cold and the life of the street that alienates her at the same time as it attracts her. Nadia has a public persona, working in a café where she seems most comfortable, meeting strangers in crowded bars, and she is the character in the film that walks the streets of London, preferring this to taking the tube. That Nadia is alone in the crowd is emphasised by Winterbottom's use of blurred-motion footage as she walks through Soho and as she catches the bus home from Tim's bedsit.

In *Wonderland* Nadia, like her two sisters, comes to us with little historical background. The looseness of the narrative provides for as many ellipses as it does explanations of character. They are little more than the character types of documentary film. Debbie is the promiscuous single mother seeking some respite from her hairdressing work and home life with her son Jack and the separation from Dan. Molly (Molly Parker) is a very pregnant aspirant, whose grumpiness is the target of her sisters' criticism, and who offers little support to her depressed husband Eddie. Despite the implied relationships, we are given little indication, other than a general sketching of familial tension, of what drove Darren (Enzo Cilenti) from home, of the difficulties of Debbie and Dan's marriage, and of the unhappiness of Eileen, Bill and Franklyn (David Fahm). Much of the film's rendering of these characters is undertaken through mise-en-scène, costuming and performance. The apparent self-assurance of Donna is relayed through her swagger, laughter and her general bearing. She has difficulties with Franklyn's introversion, and it may be that her flirtation with Bill is an indication of her loneliness (no partner is indicated), but her interaction with Bill serves to highlight *his* loneliness rather than hers. Shepherd, in this role, is the embodiment of repression, suffering his wife's abuse and lack of affection. His dull-toned voice and blank expression evoke an English working-class character type long represented in British cinema.

These characters embody personas closer to types than to the full and rounded characterisations expected from much commercial cinema. Winterbottom's characters are vehicles for the stories that reverberate between them and their surroundings. Samantha Morton, who plays Maria Gonzalez in *Code 46*, understands Winterbottom's method and perhaps his choice of her for this role:

> I think that often in film people recreate a natural environment. They'll put you on a street with extras [and say] 'Walk down that street and look

natural'. Backdrops are dead, it's very contrived, it's very controlled. And I don't think I'm a very good actor. I think I'm far better at re-acting to my environment and stimuli whether it's fellow actors or a cinematographer that I'm getting a vibe with. So what Michael did [for *Code 46*] was throw us into the real world and say, 'Perform in that environment', which I'm completely comfortable with and have done many times before.[10]

Following Laurence Coriat's ideas for the stories to be interwoven, Winterbottom involved the actors in three months of pre-production in an admixture of location-scouting and rehearsal:

To work like this the actors have to feel very comfortable with their characters. So, during rehearsal we spent a lot of time with them in the places they live. The actors were involved whilst we were choosing their flat or house to prepare for their roles. They went to work in the café or the shop. They bought stuff for their homes which were used for props or bought their clothes as costumes and so on. We tried to let the actors control their characters as much as possible ... If you make a film with a different method, you obviously hope that it will change the nature of the film itself. Because we had no lights, we were using a hand held camera, and were shooting on 16 mm, we were able to run scenes for a long time, allowing the actors to just see what happened and react to that. There was a script and then we'd carry on from that point, sometimes we would use the script to get a sense of what the scene was about, sometimes some of the actors would stick exactly to the script. But certainly there was more freedom than we would normally be able to have on a film set and we shot a lot of film. Often we would shoot for 10 minutes, then stop and just talk about the over-all scene and what was happening, then go again, rather than worry about specific details of performance.[11]

The screenplay for *Wonderland* also developed along the lines of a 'plan-of-action' script. Coriat evolved a story inspired by Robert Altman's *Short Cuts* (1993). He explains:

I liked the idea of writing a set of different interweaving stories all set in one place. I also really wanted to do a story about London because I haven't seen a film yet that looks at all the different sides to that city. I was born in France and think that, as an outsider, I have a different perspective. Outsiders usually pick up on things that others maybe don't ... I had always thought of Michael to direct this because I like his sense of aesthetics. It may be that I'm French and I like the New Wave approach to film-making. Michael is one of the few English directors who can capture that raw, documentary feel. In fact there are many parallels between *Wonderland* and a French film.[12]

Whatever its echoes and affiliations, *Wonderland* emerges as a humanist masterpiece of British cinema, bleak in many of its insights but ultimately holding out the prospect of hope for its beleaguered protagonists. As Nadia and Franklyn walk off together at the end, Winterbottom seems to be suggesting the possibility, fragile but palpable, of kindly friendship at least. They move away from the camera but forward as they make their way to work, and one is left to reflect that not all the movement that characterises Winterbottom's films, and this one specifically, is dangerous or melancholy.

24 Hour Party People

This film is discussed in more detail in chapter 5, but some aspects of it are worth noting briefly here. Like all these films *24 Hour Party People* insists upon location-shooting, episodic and elliptical narrative, and the use of non-actors. Perhaps of all Winterbottom's films, *24 Hour Party People* is the most concerned with location, in that the film is a documentary-like argument about the vitality and cultural importance of Manchester. In fact, it is as much *about* Manchester as anything else, as much as, say, Ian Curtis and Shaun Ryder, or Tony Wilson or Factory records. If anything, the film is about all these things because it is about Manchester. The Factory phenomenon, including the role played by Tony Wilson, the film insists, occurred because of the ingenuity of these Mancunians, but also because the protagonists behind the film, Winterbottom and Eaton, both from the Manchester area, had grown up with the historical Mancunian figures that populate the film: Tony Wilson, Christopher Eccleston, Paul Ryder, Mark E. Smith, Howard Devoto, Vini Reilly, Martin Hannett, Joy Division and New Order. In terms of Winterbottom's *oeuvre*, the soundtracks to his films have featured Manchester bands, such as New Order, The Stone Roses and The Happy Mondays, as early as *Butterfly Kiss*, *With or Without You* and *Welcome to Sarajevo* (New Order's 'World in Motion' is repeated from *Butterfly Kiss*).

The film also makes much of the landscape surrounding Manchester and of the urban centre. These usages include the opening scenes of Wilson hang-gliding in the Pennines, mimicking the British realist film tradition of the long shot of the town, as well as when Martin Hannett (Andy Serkis) is imaged 'recording silence' or when Tony Wilson (Steve Coogan) and Lindsay (Shirley Henderson) are looking out over the countryside. Characteristically, the film is concerned with the urban environment that produced the likes of Ian Curtis and Shaun Ryder. The film includes many night-time helicopter shots of the city, a metonymic representation of the subject of the film. Like *Welcome to*

Sarajevo and *Rome, Open City*, *24 Hour Party People* employs a grab-bag of footage, particularly in the early parts of the film. Thus we have the reconstruction of the legendary Sex Pistols' gig at the Lesser Free Trade Hall in Manchester on 4 June 1976, which melds actual 8mm footage of the event with Wilson's commentary concerning the influence of that gig, while he himself witnesses and participates in it. This sequence is followed by one in which Wilson argues the significance of his own *So It Goes* television show, a Manchester regional programme that featured the latest punk groups, and we again see footage of Siouxsie and the Banshees, Iggy Pop, The Jam and The Stranglers in concert, but also with Wilson and his friends in the crowd. In this instance *24 Hour Party People* mixes 8mm and television with Robby Müller and Marcel Zyskind's digital video footage.

The inclusion of Wilson and his friends in the historical sequence of now-legendary punk bands in performance bestows on Wilson and the others the status of 'historical' figures themselves, giving weight to the film's argument about the importance of the Factory milieu – and therefore of Manchester – to history, but also making these events themselves historically significant in a broader sense. The film invites us to understand the micro-historical events in relation to the larger event of Thatcherism and its social and cultural consequences. Part of this invitation is to assert the importance of Manchester, a provincial metropolis of the UK, as an important cultural centre utilising the found footage and re-enactment for its documentary efficacy.

The Road to Guantánamo

In Winterbottom's *The Road to Guantánamo* it is possible to see a movement from the re-enactment format of *In This World* to docu-drama. Like *In This World*, *The Road to Guantánamo* is based on contemporary historical events and here it derives from a particular controversial effect of the so-called 'war on terror'. This is the case of Ruhel Ahmed, Shafiq Rasul and Asif Iqbal, three British nationals who came to be known as the Tipton Three after their hometown in the West Midlands, not far from Birmingham. All assert that that they were in Pakistan for Asif Iqbal to get married and, later, in Afghanistan to assist the local population in charity work during the initial US bombing campaigns. Arrested in Afghanistan, the three were imprisoned in the United States detainment camp at Guantánamo Bay, Cuba, established for suspects in the 'war on terror' following the bombings in the US on 11 September 2001.

The film is a combination of drama, direct-address interview and found footage. The film combines Mat Whitecross's interview footage with Ruhel Ahmed, Shafiq Rasul and Asif Iqbal recounting stories of their experience and the *performance* of these stories with Farhad Harun as Ruhel, Rizwan Ahmed as Shafiq and Arfan Usman as Asif. Waqar Siddiqui plays the other member of their initial party, Monir, who is not interviewed because he disappeared while in Afghanistan. Among these two aspects, the film employs footage from Al Jazeera, the BBC, ITN Archive and AP Television to contextualise these events within larger political shifts, indicated by speeches from George Bush Jr., President of the United States, and Donald Rumsfeld, United States Secretary of Defence.

Shot in the United Kingdom, Pakistan, Afghanistan and Iran, *The Road to Guantánamo* follows many of the structures, motifs and aesthetics of *In This World*. Like *In This World* it was shot on digital video on locations near where the actual events took place. Obviously the scenes set in the Camps X-Ray and Delta in Cuba were not shot there; they were filmed in Iran, and reinforced with images of these camps from the news services. Andrew Eaton elucidates:

> There were logical reasons behind it. First of all, unlike Pakistan or Afghanistan, Iran has got a fairly strong indigenous film industry, so you're going to a place where there are plenty of technicians and people who have a lot of experience. We also had a good relationship with the line producer [Mike Elliott] there. We needed to be in a place that would work as a good match for Afghanistan, geographically, and also a place where we'd be able to find the right ethnic mix of extras. To re-enact the war in Afghanistan on the scale we wanted would have been dangerous and politically sensitive [sic] to do in Pakistan.[13]

Echoing the pre-production of *In This World*, Winterbottom had Wendy Brazington visit a number of schools and colleges in Birmingham to locate the actors to play Ruhel, Shafiq, Asif and Monir. Rizwan Ahmed, who plays Shafiq, had just graduated from a drama school, while the others had no acting experience.[14] There is some physical dissimilarity between the interviewees and their dramatic doubles, and the film's eschewal of physical likeness creates some initial confusion, reinforcing the notion that Ruhel, Shafiq, Asif and Monir are everyday people caught up in confusing and intricate events. This strategy implied that these characters could be any of us, innocent people caught up in historical events. The confusion for the spectator of, for example, who is playing Ruhel, only adds to the alarming whirl of incidents in which they are embroiled. The performances are like an exposition of the stories that the interviewees tell. Part of the function of these non-actors is to invite the spectator to identify closely with their plight. As with *In This World*, the film argues that they are innocent and that they don't deserve to be treated as they are.

Like *In This World*, *The Road to Guantánamo* is part-road movie. The first part of the film, prior to the boys being captured by the Northern Alliance forces, is a journey into the bewildering world of the Middle East. Many of the problems that the boys face, and that form part of their case, grow out of their unfamiliarity with the geography of Pakistan and Afghanistan, and this leads to their being captured and wrongly accused. This notion is played out in two scenes. The first of these is when they reach the border between Pakistan and Afghanistan. Because of his gastroenteritis Shafiq, who is detained in the toilet at a mosque, is left behind when the boys are journeying to Afghanistan. We are told that the initial bus driver 'hit someone' and then ran off, stranding the bus and its passengers, until another driver is found and a change of buses. As the other three ride the bus, Shafiq implores people to give him a lift to the border but eventually he simply walks across the border until he meets up with his friends who have crossed as pillion passengers on motorbikes. In the interview, Shafiq recalls, 'I ended up walking across the border. No one stopped me'. This sequence is made up of footage from different sources, angles and shot scales. The filmmakers shot the scene at a market in Afghanistan, mixing their footage of the actors on motorbikes and shots of Rizwan Ahmed (as Shafiq) walking among the crowds with the footage from the news services, accompanied by a voice-over from the BBC about the brave Afghan aid workers. The images of Pakistan are sun-filled and full of colour compared with the foreboding of the vistas of a misty Afghanistan, the latter eventually merging into images of darkness and of the boys' first encounter with the bombing campaign there. The second sequence occurs when the boys reach Kabul and, after about two-and-a-half weeks of inactivity owing to the bombing and with Asif ill, they decide to return to Pakistan. They find themselves at the mercy of a mini-bus driver who, unbeknown to them, takes them in the wrong direction, and eventually to a house in Kunduz where they are captured with many Taliban fighters. Winterbottom elides completely this journey from Kabul in the east to Kunduz, in contrast with the detailed rendering of the journey taken from Quetta in Pakistan.

The Road to Guantánamo is an elliptical journey from Tipton, Birmingham to Karachi, Quetta, Kandahar, Kabul, Kunduz, Camp X-ray, and Camp Delta and back to the UK. Like *In This World*, *The Road to Guantánamo* is a combination of drama and documentary. It is the function of the interview materials in relation to the dramatic episodes which distinguishes the effect of *The Road to Guantánamo* from *In This*

World. In this way the film is closer to the docu-drama form than *In This World* is.

John Corner, in *The Art of Record*, distinguishes between the 'documentary-drama' and the 'dramatised documentary'.[15] The former 'is seen to develop a documentary character either as a result of its scale of referentiality to specific real events (private or public or both), or because of its manner of depiction'.[16] The latter 'begins with the documentary base or core and uses dramatisation to overcome certain limitations and to achieve a more broadly popular and imaginatively powerful effect'.[17] Corner's distinction enables us better to understand the differences between *In This World* and *The Road to Guantánamo*. *In This World* is a re-enactment of imagined historical events. The journeying of Jamal and Enayatullah is not a re-enactment of a specific series of private events but a journey undertaken by the characters (and the 'social actors' portraying them) on behalf of the film. In this way the events that occur are for the most part fictional, or are both fictional and actual, occurring while in the act of making a fictional narrative. As with the 'plan-of action script' mentioned earlier, the conditions of production infect the fiction. *In This World* also gives to this fiction a documentary quality. This is done through the use of Paul Popplewell's narration and the already mentioned use of maps and titles of cities. Following Corner, this kind of referentiality, involving the real-life historical people-smuggling that is known to occur regularly in all parts of the world, and the re-enactment of the methods in the historical world in Winterbottom's film, turns the fiction into a documentary-drama. *The Road to Guantánamo*, again following Corner's distinction, can be considered a dramatised-documentary. The initial part of the production involved Mat Whitecross spending 'about a month in a house interviewing' the protagonists, which meant the production team has 650 pages of transcribed material with which to fashion the re-enactment of their stories.[18] This 'documentary' accounting for the events sets the basis for the film to which are added the dramatic episodes to overcome the limitations of the interview mode of storytelling. In this way *The Road to Guantánamo* follows the melodramatic form, imploring us to identify with Ruhel, Shafiq and Asif, and to a lesser extent Monir, as innocent people caught up in larger historical events.

The use of news footage not only contextualises the smaller episodes of the boys' journey, but also provides an ironic tone from which to understand the invasion of Afghanistan in relation to the boys' story. Winterbottom was asked why he employed the news footage:

> Partly as a way of helping the narration, because all of us saw what was happening in Afghanistan through the news, so to remind people what

was going on. Partly to contrast between their experiences on the ground as three individuals caught up in it compared to watching it from the outside. On a slightly more specific basis, virtually all the news that we were seeing was from the point of view of the cameras and news crews who were with the Americans or the Northern Alliance. They weren't in places where our guys were. So you get a double perspective – them on the ground being bombed as opposed to reporters with the guys doing the bombing. And also using newsreel helped us tell the story as quickly and simply as possible.[19]

This economy of narration to which Winterbottom alludes compresses the historical events as described by the interviewees, fantastic as they are, and renders the grander pronouncements of George Bush and Donald Rumsfeld as incommensurate with the boys' stories that we are hearing and witnessing.

The ironic 'disconnection' between the large historical events that we know and have come to understand through our experience of the reports from reporters, combined with the intimate personal accounts from the interviewees, both impact on the re-enacted episodes to 'reduce' the story of the Tipton Three to the realms of the everyday, far removed from the fantastic images of large-scale bombings, speeches and the, by now, familiar rhetoric of war. Like *In This World* and *Welcome to Sarajevo*, *The Road to Guantánamo* insists on getting beneath these images to counterbalance them with the smaller, intimate episodes of everyday life. Winterbottom describes his approach to the film:

One of the most striking things about them, and something that we wanted to show people was that they were just ordinary British teenagers who got caught up in these events. We were all told that the people in Guantánamo were the most dangerous terrorists in the world, and that's why it was necessary for America to create this bizarre extra-legal prison, and when we met them they were so ordinary. So we wanted them to show the gap between what you thought people would be like in Guantánamo and the reality of meeting them. The simplest and most effective way to tell their story was to have them tell it within the film.[20]

Why *In This World*?

Given our earlier mention of Roberto Rossellini, there is no escaping a consideration of the title of Winterbottom's refugee drama. *In This World* signifies not only the moral question posed by the narrative of the film but also that posed by the qualities of films related formally and philosophically to neo-realism. Winterbottom's *oeuvre* constitutes a contemporary moral voice in troubled times. Again and again his dramas, and even his comedies, pose moral dilemmas that implore their audiences to consider the contexts – that is, the *worlds* – from which they emerge. The ultimate question related to *Welcome to Sarajevo*, *In This World* and *The Road to Guantánamo* is how can we, the audience, allow these events to occur in this world? How can people use each other so carelessly as they do in *Wonderland*? For *24 Hour Party People* the question posed is: Did we know that these kinds of things happen in this world? This is a question of unofficial history, micro-histories of unofficial cultures of Manchester and post-punk. The film's Tony Wilson, like Michael Henderson in *Welcome to Sarajevo* or Jamal and Enayatullah in *In This World* or Ruhel, Shafiq and Asif in *The Road to Guantánamo*, is an historical figure, not a real-life person but a figure subject to the felicities or otherwise of the culture to which each belongs (as indeed are the unhappy sisters in *Wonderland*). Winterbottom's realist worlds emphasise this and the conditions, filmic and otherwise, that make this possible.

Notes

1 Michael Winterbottom, quoted in the *In This World* Press Kit, p. 5.
2 Wendy Brazington, quoted in the *In This World* Press Kit, p. 9.
3 *Ibid.*
4 Jean Douchet, *French New Wave*, p. 186.
5 Toni Grisoni, *In This World* Press Kit, pp. 7–8.
6 Michel Marie, *The French New Wave*, pp. 77–8.
7 Rossellini quoted in Marie, *The French New Wave*, p. 68.
8 Michael Atkinson, 'Cinema as Art Attack', *Film Comment*, 34 (January/February 1998), p. 45.
9 Michael Winterbottom, 'Interview', *Wonderland* Press Kit, p. 8.
10 Samantha Morton in 'Obtaining Cover', *Code 46* DVD.
11 Winterbottom, *Wonderland* Press Kit, p. 6.
12 Laurence Coriat, quoted in *Wonderland* Press Kit, p. 3.
13 Andrew Eaton, 'Interview', *The Road to Guantánamo* Press Kit. p. 16
14 *Ibid.*
15 John Corner, *The Art of Record: A Critical Introduction to Documentary* (Manchester: Manchester University Press, 1996), p. 34.
16 *Ibid.*
17 *Ibid.*
18 Michael Winterbottom, 'Interview', *The Road to Guantánamo* Press Kit, p. 10.
19 *Ibid*, p. 11.
20 *Ibid*, p. 10.

The adaptor:
Winterbottom and the English novel 4

It is unlikely that anyone is ever going to label Winterbottom as a 'literary director'. Though he has adapted three major English novels to the screen within the space of a decade, and though there is a very long tradition of British filmmakers' falling back on adapting the classics, *faute de mieux*, Winterbottom scarcely seems to belong in the same camp as such illustrious adaptors as David Lean or Anthony Asquith. Or, nearer the present, one doesn't think of him in the same breath as Merchant Ivory or even Iain Softley, whose version of *The Wings of the Dove* (1997, screenplay by Hossein Amini, who wrote *Jude*) set a new standard in British cinema for the adaptation enterprise. There is certainly nothing decorous about his approach to the classics of English literature; his films are not examples of starry casts comporting themselves before listed buildings. However they start out, they end up as Winterbottom films. Those who admired his first cinema feature, *Butterfly Kiss* or the subsequent telemovie *Go Now*, a wracking study in degenerative illness, would not have been likely to expect him next to turn his interests and talents to adapting Thomas Hardy's late Victorian tragic novel, *Jude the Obscure*. Since then, of course, one has been led to expect of Winterbottom not to be surprised at any turn his career might take.

Jude

The first of his literary adaptations was *Jude*, and following, as it did, his *Butterfly Kiss*, it seemed almost as much road movie as film version of classic novel. As a French critic at the time wrote: 'S'il respecte la succession des lieux choisie par Hardy comme structure, *Jude* ne reproduit pas servilement le matériau littéraire' ['If he respects the series of places chosen by Hardy as a structure, *Jude* doesn't slavishly reproduce the literary material'];[1] the comment recognises both Winterbottom's approach to adaptation and the road movie element. We have argued elsewhere that one of the characterising traits of a Winterbottom film is his urge towards constant movement, both of characters and of the camera that records them. Reviewing *Jude* at the time of its release Brian McFarlane wrote: 'On the evidence of the genuinely alarming *Butterfly Kiss*, one would not have expected him to prettify a tough novel or to fall into a consciously literary style of filmmaking. It is good to report that he has avoided both traps'.[2] A decade later the individuality and the making of rigorous choices seem even more obvious, though the film failed commercially. Not surprising perhaps, because *Jude* is after all one of the darkest of all Victorian novels, even for the relentlessly fatalistic, downbeat Hardy.

The film opens on a bleak landscape over which the light slowly passes. Shot in black-and-white, this opening sequence establishes at once a mood of foreboding that recalls *Butterfly Kiss* rather than, say, *Howards End* (1992), with a feel not of the Home Counties but of some much more daunting terrain. In fact, though the film is set in Hardy's 'Wessex', Winterbottom has ventured further afield in his quest for more demanding locations which he found in Yorkshire, and even Hardy's 'Christminster', goal of Jude's aspirations, is evoked by Edinburgh rather than its actual and mellower real-life counterpart, Oxford. It is worth noting this at the outset because it suggests that the director is more concerned with emotional essentials than with mere authenticity in relation to the original novel. As well, Winterbottom has chosen to open with Jude himself rather than by way of Phillotson's departure and Jude's reaction to this: this is only a matter of emphasis, but it works to put Jude at once at the centre of the narrative.

In the rest of this monochrome introduction, the young Jude Fawley (James Daley) is seen walking down the straight furrows of the fields frightening off the birds. The straightness of the furrows may seem to posit a sense of direction – or they may seem, in hindsight, to mock his schoolmaster's words to him at the end of this prologue: 'You can choose your future'. Choice is what will again and again be denied to Jude. These long overhead shots of the hillside fields alert the viewer at once to the idea of a world view in which people are dwarfed by their circumstances, and in this matter many of Winterbottom's films share an attitude with Hardy. (Think of the rescued child in *Welcome to Sarajevo* or the refugees in *In This World*, for examples.) Jude is bullied in the fields by the farmer for feeding the rooks he is meant to be dispersing, and there is a harsh image of a half-dozen dead birds hanging from a pole in the field, 'an intimation of the tragic events ahead' as Geoffrey Macnab has noted.[3]

From the start, then, Jude's compassion is represented as being at odds with the harsher realities of his world. This is not a benign landscape and the village to which Jude runs home, Marygreen, is a sodden, gloomy set of stone houses, more oppressive than picturesque. In the atmosphere of qualified pastoral evoked in these opening sequences, Winterbottom recalls such earlier British films as Lance Comfort's *Great Day* (1945) or *Bang! You're Dead* (1953) and Ken Loach's *Kes* (1969): there has been a thin but tenacious tendency in British filmmaking to resist 'temptations to sentimentalise the rural landscape', being 'careful to register its austerities as well as its serenities'.[4]

As well as the figure-in-a-landscape aspect of this opening, Winterbottom also introduces two other thematic concerns that will preoccupy his protagonist. When Jude returns to the home of the aunt (June Whitfield) with whom he lives, she reproaches him for letting the farmer bully him. 'His father was my father's journeyman', she says, almost in an aside but enough for us to register a community in which class will matter at all sorts of levels. The other crucial matter is that already hinted at above. Phillotson (Liam Cunningham), Jude's teacher, is leaving the village and, as he and Jude are silhouetted on the cart bearing his belongings away, they stop on the brow of a hill facing Christminster in the distance. Phillotson tells Jude: 'If you want to do anything in life, that's where you have to go', outlining the challenges and rigours of the scholar's life. As if to dramatise the romantic nature of Jude's aspirations as he listens, the camera turns to view the distant, gleaming prospect of Christminster, recalling Oxford's 'dreaming spires', in Arnold's phrase,[5] and subdued colour seeps into the scene.

The colour is delusive though. Jude has not been able to choose his future and the second movement of the film enacts the start of his entrapment by circumstances. He has become not a scholar but a stonemason. In the brief glimpse of the grown Jude (Christopher Eccleston) at his trade and with his fellow workmen, however, Winterbottom is astute enough not to reveal this as mere oppressiveness. He is at ease with them and with his work, and with dedication rather than resentment goes off to a secluded riverbank to read the classics, having taught himself some Greek and Latin. His absorption in his reading is shattered by a hunk of pig's innards being thrown at him by Arabella (Rachel Griffiths), who, with two friends, is preparing the animal's body for eating. Arabella, in a red skirt, her bare legs visible as she sits carelessly on a rock in the water, is at once associated with the opulence of nature, giggling 'Hoity-toity' when Jude tells her what he is reading. She offers and he cannot resist the crudely physical temptation of easily won gratification. Her raw sensuality and the voluptuous curve of her breasts make powerful appeal to him and the film cuts to a Breughe-lesque marriage celebration in which the high-spirited bride leads the chase after a piglet. Sexual exigency will ruin Jude's life. When his aunt quietly reproaches him for being entrapped into marrying Arabella, who has proved not to be pregnant, he says, echoing Phillotson, 'I had no choice'. One recalls in this regard the opening sequence in which he got his ears boxed for exercising choice in feeding the birds.

The rest of his life will bear witness to the way his paths are deter-mined by forces other than his own aspirations. At the heart of Jude's story is a study in conflicting desires: between the life of the mind and spirit on the one hand and, on the other, the raw demands of the life of the senses. The film, generally hewing close to the novel's sombre trajec-tory, makes clear that, in the articulation of these conflicting forces, Jude has no more choice than he had in his doomed marriage to Arabella. He will be thwarted in both sets of aspirations/impulses/desires. The conflict is not an especially rare one; what gives it its tragic power is Jude's intensity, which finds a brilliant incarnation in Eccleston's perfor-mance, as he tries to maintain integrity of purpose and action in the face of what come to seem the universe's malign plans for him. And Eccleston's bony, ascetic, intelligent face makes him ideal casting in physical terms: he *looks* like an aspirant.

The feeling of frustration so central to Jude's story is underlined in the film by its sense of constant movement which seems to mock the attempts at realising aspirations. The more Jude moves, the less prog-ress he seems to make. Winterbottom has, quite boldly, retained the section headings of the novel: At Marygreen, At Christminster, and so on. 'Boldly' because this might have led critics to assume a leaden fidelity to the original when this is not in fact what he offers at all. What these titles, starkly given in white lettering on a black screen, do is to insist on the journey aspect of the narrative, not just in physical terms but also in relation to the bleak journey of Jude's life. It is not exactly a road movie in the way that *Butterfly Kiss* more clearly is (though even there it is generically crossed with *amour fou*). However, 'Jude's career is marked by pounding journeys' as one writer has said;[6] and, in its numerous images of trains cutting through the countryside or of Jude trudging uphill to find Sue at Shaston as others run cheerily down or of Jude and his little family tramping through the sodden Christminster streets in search of accommodation, it keeps recalling Winterbottom's preceding study of doomed lives. Trevor Waite's editing several times cuts to a moving train while the soundtrack refers to some past event such as a letter he is reading from or retains the previous image while ushering in the next move via the sound of the train. The effect of continuity of movement signified in such editorial practices is then frequently undercut, between episodes, by the use of fades, which suggests an arbitrary *dis*continuity of experience, as if, for all their apparently kinetic qualities, these are lives always in danger of losing their momentum.

The 'dreaming spires' of Jude's first distant glimpse of Christminster, the focus for his intellectual and spiritual yearnings, dissolve into a grimmer reality up close. Winterbottom, rejecting the honeyed hues of Oxford and, with his great cinematographer, Eduardo Serra, using Edinburgh for grimmer effect, has established a powerful image of the place as the scene of chilly architecture and an intellectual life from which Jude is excluded. There are poignant images of Jude as he watches while passing gowned scholars go heedlessly about their way. This effect is even more heart-rending when Jude returns to Christminster much later in time to see the august procession of scholars, in relation to whom he knows himself now to be inevitably, and in perpetuity, an outsider. It is as though the cold dismissiveness of the letter of rejection from the Dean of Admissions, smugly advising Jude that he will have 'more chance of success in sticking to your own trade', however meanly class-based, has proved no more than the truth.

Whereas a serious 'heritage' film would never have resisted the lure of Oxford's colleges and quads, Winterbottom wants us to see Jude's ideal as delusive. This is the place in which Phillotson, Jude's old teacher and mentor, has given up on his intellectual ambitions and settled for modest school-teaching, instead of the scholarly career he had in mind, and rain is characteristically bucketing down as Jude goes to renew his acquaintance with him. Jude is prepared to wait, to teach himself to read the classics of the ancient world, and he demonstrates his facility by reciting the Creed in Latin in a pub before an audience of raucous undergraduates, whose privileges he will never share. In keeping with Hardy's perception of how Christminster and the intellectual life have failed Jude, Winterbottom resists the clichés of the heritage school of filmmaking in depicting the university city, and equally he resists the temptation to turn Phillotson into a caricature of desiccation. Cunningham plays him as a disappointed, not unattractive man in early middle-age, who has settled for the possible, and whose failure to distinguish himself in Christminster prefigures Jude's own more profound failure.

The film deals brilliantly with the other side of Jude's nature – with the demands of the sensual life. The two actresses, Rachel Griffiths as Arabella and Kate Winslet as Sue Bridehead, are very aptly cast and create not just contrasting figures in an emotional diagram (as they sometimes seem in Hardy's novel) but two rounded characters. Part of their skill –

and of Hossein Amini's screenplay – in this regard is to soften the edges of schematism by giving them both a firm physicality and suggesting a shared vacillation, albeit from different motives. Whereas Arabella is impelled essentially by selfishness, she is also allowed a valuable instinct for survival, and this, allied to her obvious sensuality, accounts for her dodging in and out of Jude's life, usually to herald some new disaster for him. Griffiths has no trouble in suggesting the raw, heedless sexuality but she also embeds it in a fully realised whole. Her dishonesties are on the surface and their aim is to keep her afloat in a none too easy world. When Winterbottom contrasts the way Jude shies away from killing a pig with Arabella's going at it as if all in a day's work, the image acknowledges both her moral crudity and a sort of necessary pragmatism. Jude pores over his books while the practical Arabella hangs and guts the pig. In all, Winterbottom's concept of Arabella, articulated in the details of Griffiths's performance, is a more generous, perhaps juster, appraisal of the type than Hardy has allowed. One commentator, the director/writer Philip Goodhew, remarked aptly: 'Rachel Griffiths actually improves on the blowsy tart without a heart of the novel by cleverly eschewing the easy options and playing her as an intelligent, pragmatic woman who plays the establishment game to her own ends'.[7]

As for Winslet's Sue, she is every bit as irritating as Hardy's but again the film allows her a kind of direct sexual energy that unites her at one level with Arabella. However, whereas Arabella's notion is to make sexual energy work for her, Sue's sensuality is always at the mercy of her 'modern manners'. It is hard to see why Winterbottom and Amini decided to include the claptrap about how Jude should avoid contact with his cousin Sue because of a family curse that accounts for how 'The Fawleys were not made for wedlock: it never seemed to sit well upon us'.[8] Winslet's complexly detailed performance provides quite enough evidence for the difficulties in the way of a tranquil future for her and Jude, quite apart from *external* difficulties like his foolish marriage to Arabella and Sue's even more foolish one to Phillotson. Winslet not merely conveys the twists and turns in Sue's ways of assessing her experience, both emotional and intellectual, but she is also as sensually ripe a figure as Griffiths. When she buys a naked male statuette at a market, she is clearly making a statement that is both aesthetic and sexual. Compared with the gaunt, serious face of Eccleston's Jude, hers is full, ripe and seems, unlike his, to be suppressing nothing.

When she asks him, 'Do I irritate you?', it is as though she is aware of her own complexity. She reminds one of just how important a figure she is in Victorian literature, poised as she is near the turn of the century. She now seems a natural literary forebear of such women as Lawrence's

Gudrun Brangwen: reading *Women in Love* with *Jude* in mind, one can't help thinking of her as a case of Sue Bridehead Revisited. It is harder for a film to do justice to Sue's studied intellectual iconoclasm than to the sensual and emotional aspects of the character, but Macnab is surely right when he writes that 'Kate Winslet, outstanding as Jude's fiercely idealistic cousin, starts in an exuberant groove, but by the final reel is almost mute with suffering'.[9] Sue, with her maddening switches of allegiance, with her febrile moral imagination, is, on paper at least, a hard heroine to warm to, and the film doesn't shirk such obstacles to empathy with her. In fact, after the deaths of their children and Jude's son by Arabella, she is given the following non-Hardy dialogue which severely tests our engagement with her even in her grief. As she packs to leave Jude, she says: 'Your child killed mine. How can I live with you? How can I look at you?' Following the infant tragedy, Sue moves towards the conformism she has so often scoffed at and returns to Phillotson.

The film moves inexorably, as the novel does, towards its bleak denouement, stopping short of the death of Jude with which Hardy concludes his agonising fable of lives crushed by a heartless and intransigent society – as well as by a malign fate. But if Winterbottom spares us the death, his film's last moments are still about as heart-wrenching as they could be. On Christmas Day 1889, Jude goes into the empty snow-covered streets of Christminster, then to the graveyard where Sue is kneeling by the children's grave. The scene is almost drained of colour, recalling the grim monochrome opening sequence, as they kiss passionately, followed by her striding off to leave him alone there. He shouts, 'We are man and wife if ever two people were on this earth', and the camera pulls up with Jude left standing alone in the snowy cemetery. The pain of this ending is in the hopelessness of love denied in the interests of a misguided moral system and in the refusal of mutual comfort between two who have been buffeted almost beyond bearing. Roger Ebert, characterising Winterbottom as 'angry, clear-headed, and with a sure visual sense', rightly claims that 'his casting gives personalities to the characters ... Together they [Eccleston, Winslet and Griffiths] take a difficult story and make it into a haunting film'.[10]

Jude has an impeccable sense of period and place but Winterbottom never allows his cameraman or his designers to clog the narrative with the sort of detail that sometimes evokes delighted recognition of its mere authenticity. There is never any sense of jarring about when and where the story is set; this information is taken for granted as if it were a contemporary tale. What clearly matters more to the director is how the look and movement of the film reflect the inevitable, bruising tragedy of lives that never get to make the 'choices' they want.

The Claim

If *Jude* is a rigorous confrontation of a very demanding novel, staking its claim to originality on its refusal of the novel's schematism and on rounding out characters and situations that might seem to reflect this tendency, Winterbottom's next adaptation was an altogether more radical departure from its literary source. There is surely a degree of conceptual daring and imaginative fluidity in relocating *The Mayor of Casterbridge* to the Sierra Nevadas, California, and in effect making a Western of it. In fact, it was filmed in the Fortress Mountain area of Alberta, Canada, and, as one writer has noted, 'the severity of this climate registers in nearly every shot', going on to suggest that 'the snow is a character here [in *The Claim*] – as much as the sun and the desert at the end of Erich von Stroheim's *Greed*'.[11]

It is not, though, just a matter of setting the story in America, and thereby in a way following up the intentions of Hardy's young Donald Farfrae, thwarted by Mayor Michael Henchard, who persuades him to give up the idea of America and to settle in Casterbridge, a decision both will come to regret bitterly. It is, as well, a matter of fully re-imagining how the emotional trajectories which constitute Hardy's plot might be reassembled, within both the settings and the generic characteristics of a long-established Hollywood mode. In terms of iconography, narrative incident and motifs, character types and ideology, Winterbottom's film emerges at least as much a Western as an adaptation of Hardy.

The film opens on a vast snowy landscape as a wagonload of people arrives at Kingdom Come, an isolated mining town of timber build-ings picturesquely if precariously perched in a declivity of the Sierra Nevadas, the year given as 1867 – that is, the period of post-Civil War reconstruction, which is reputedly the most popular for the Hollywood Western. The awesome bleakness recalls the opening sequence of Winterbottom's *Jude*, in fact, it almost looks as if it is shot in black and white; but it also recalls that masterly revisionist Western of the early 1970s, Robert Altman's *McCabe and Mrs Miller*. This is a comparison to which this study will return on several counts, including the welcoming profession of the 'ladies'. The town has a no-firearms rule, on the orders of Mr Dillon (Peter Mullan) who runs it, and, in the tradition of the classic Western narrative paradigm, the status quo is about to be disturbed by the arrival of strangers in the town. These are Dalglish (Wes Bentley), who has come to talk business matters with Dillon, and mother and daughter, Elena and Hope Burn (Nastassja Kinski and Sarah Polley). Already installed is the brothel-keeper, Lucia (Milla Jovovich), and the five chief counterparts of Hardy's tale – Henchard/Dillon, Farfrae/Dalglish, Susan/Elena, Elizabeth-Jane/Hope, and Lucetta/Lucia – are quickly in place. Standing in for Hardy's large supporting cast of villagers and townspeople are miners, railroad workers, prostitutes and various other employees of Dillon.

In a Preface to the first edition of *The Mayor of Casterbridge*, Hardy wrote that:

> The incidents narrated arise mainly out of three events ... in the real history of the town called Casterbridge and the neighbouring country. They were the sale of a wife by her husband, the uncertain harvests which immediately preceded the repeal of the Corn Laws, and the visit of a Royal personage to the aforesaid part of England.[12]

Winterbottom and his screenwriter Frank Cottrell Boyce (seven-times collaborator of the director) have used only the first of these 'incidents', though the other two have semi-parallels, as we shall see. Even in relation to the wife-selling, the filmmakers have chosen not to begin their narrative with so bizarre and striking an event but only to reveal it gradually in a series of flashbacks, or, more accurately, memory sequences. As Dillon picks up the framed photograph of a man, woman and child, he recalls an arduous journey of years before, arriving in a snowstorm at Kingdom Come. In a miner's tent, the young woman breast-feeds the child, while the young man talks to a miner who shakes a bag of gold dust and fragments on a table and says: 'With no pleasure, a man loses heart – even if he makes a strike'. He needs, not more gold, but a woman. 'Take that one', says the drunk young Dillon, indicating his wife Elena. There are two further brief flashbacks that ruffle the narrative linearity of the novel: one in which the older Dillon recalls the earlier journey when Hope (whom he believes to be his daughter) recites in the saloon, and finally, when Elena is very ill, he looks reflectively from her sickroom window and remembers himself twenty years earlier yelling for Elena the day after he had sold her. What the film loses in the novel's shocking kick-start to the story it gains in the representation of Dillon: here is a man who runs a town, a man respected by all, feared by some, but who after all these years of achievement is increasingly made to confront the guilt of his past, the foolish cruelty that, brought to the surface of his mind, undermines crucially his sense of his self and what he has achieved, and that will ultimately destroy him. One reviewer evokes Dillon's shame in these words: 'winter is a time for memory and regret. Mr. Dillon did something years ago that was wrong in a way a man cannot forgive himself for. He lives in an ornate Victorian house, submits to the caresses of his mistress, settles the affairs of his subjects and is haunted by his memories'.[13]

The idea of the stranger arriving in a Western town is central to what has been called the 'classical plot' of the Western genre. Will Wright has written: 'It [the classical Western] is the story of the lone stranger who rides into a troubled town and cleans it up, winning the respect of the townsfolk and the love of the schoolmarm'.[14] Wright acknowledges that 'There are many variations on this theme' and *The Claim* exemplifies that rider. As noted above, two lots of strangers arrive at Kingdom Come, and both will disrupt the life of the man who has built it and runs it, and, in their doing so, they will also have cataclysmic effects on the town itself. The two women will, by the way their presence awakens his conscience, fatally destroy his *amour propre*. Elena, now dying, wants financial security for Hope, who is ignorant of the shameful way her parents had separated. Dillon has been engaged in a comfortable sexual relationship with the brothel-keeping Lucia who, when he offers her a 'settlement', slaps him when she accuses him of wanting 'to fuck that little girl [Hope]'. Wanting to make amends for his youthful folly – and there is a sense of large simplicity about Dillon – he 'remarries' Elena, with a celebratory dance for the wedding occasion, which echoes ironically moments in classical Westerns such as *My Darling Clementine* (1946) and any number of other John Ford films, where the celebration was more apt to be univalent.

The other stranger is the railroad engineer Dalglish, who, like Hardy's young Scot, Donald Farfrae, emerges as a man of the future, as well as being of a more equable temperament than the man who runs the town. Like Farfrae in relation to Henchard, Dalglish will challenge Dillon's authority and complacency, though in neither case is that the intention, and will become the possessor of all that once belonged to the older man. Dalglish is employed by the Central Pacific Railroad Company whose aim is to link the line from the west coast with that from the east. Attracted to Hope, he goes off to explore possible routes for the railway and his decision in this matter helps to precipitate the final fall for Dillon. This threat is encapsulated in a laconic dialogue Dalglish has with a Company executive who asks:

'What about this town, Kingdom Come?'
'They can move it.'
'Anyone gonna give you any trouble?'
'I guess so.'
'Do what you have to do.'

As in so many classical Westerns, there is inevitably a clash between established powers and the new (think of the cattle barons v. the homesteaders in *Shane*, 1952; the corporation that does for McCabe's eminence in the town of Presbyterian Church in *McCabe and Mrs Miller*). In Western lore, the railroad signifies both expansionist romance *and* a threat to those communities that will become backwaters in its wake. This is what happens to Kingdom Come. The town is moved and the Portuguese Lucia names the new town in the valley, Lisboa (a European memory?), and asserts her authority in saying to Dillon, 'No guns allowed in my town', when he has to go there to the Telegraph Office to send for a priest following Elena's death. This shift from Kingdom Come to Lisboa has not been effected without a showdown in which guns have been drawn and in which Dillon's lieutenant, Sweetley (Sean McGinley), has been killed. The inevitability of the railroad and its impact on the lives of Dillon and the town has a sort of parallel in the novel with the arrival of the horse-drill, scornfully dismissed by Henchard and embraced by Farfrae as bound to revolutionise the agricultural basis of Casterbridge's prosperity.

With Elena dead and Hope gone in search of Dalglish, and the town he has ruled now deserted, Dillon has nothing left to live for. He sets fire to Kingdom Come – and this almost monochromatic film suddenly bursts into the colour of flames (another echo of Altman's film), though quickly replaced by black smoke on the distant horizon when viewed from the bustling new town-in-the-making, Lisboa – and wanders out to die in the snow, where his body is found the next day. Dalglish talks of him, a trifle glibly but perhaps with some real appreciation, as 'a king', even as the looters move into the ruins of Kingdom Come in search of the gold bars Dillon had stashed away. The camera then pulls up very high (echoing the last moments of *Jude*) as Hope and Dalglish walk off, tiny figures in a vast landscape, thus restating visually at the end what has been a recurring motif in the film: the precarious foothold of man in an often hostile universe.

In narrative terms, then, *The Claim* fits easily into one of the dominant Western paradigms, though tonally it is closer to *McCabe and Mrs Miller*, in which Robert Altman reworked the classical lineaments to startlingly new and melancholy effect. In fact, Winterbottom and Altman share a fascination not so much with particular film genres as with the concept of genre itself, as evidenced in their way of moving from one genre to another, often with unsettling effect.[15] A stranger arrives in each of the two (religiously named) townships in remote, isolated geographical situations and in daunting weather conditions. It's interesting to note how Hardy stresses the isolation of Casterbridge as 'a place deposited in the block upon a cornfield' (p. 109). Each stranger has plans for progress and each film ends with a body frozen to death in the snow, though in *McCabe* it is the man who came as a stranger in the opening scene who lies dead, the victim of a bigger-business take-over, while in *The Claim* it is the man who has been replaced by the stranger in community esteem who is dead. In either case, it is a powerfully bleak note on which to end a film in a genre more commonly geared towards celebrating human enterprise.

It is not just in the matter of narrative that Winterbottom recalls Altman's masterpiece. In terms of its iconography, the bone-chilling wintriness of the scene creates images as memorable as those of the rain-sodden and finally snowbound vistas and township in *McCabe*; and it shares with the earlier film a resolute realism and subdued glow about its interiors that contrasts with the sudden outdoor expanses of, in this case, craggy whiteness. And this contrast reinforces others: that of quiet interiors with noisy exteriors, that of brief bursts of activity and action with moments of elegiac stillness. As with *McCabe*, the centre of warmth in the township seems to be the brothel, presided over again by a shrewd businesswoman. Whereas Mrs Miller was entrepreneurially sharper than the endearing bumbler McCabe, here Lucia, with a clear sense of where the future lies, relocates to – and names – Lisboa. In a rare comic moment she calls out to one of her girls, Annie (Shirley Henderson), to stop 'givin' it away' to Ballanger (Julian Richings), whose growing mutual love is perhaps the film's one unequivocal 'positive'. Their wedding, in the film's penultimate episode, takes place in the new town and the camera retreats from the celebration to take in the smoke rising from Kingdom Come. The sweet-tempered pair are firmly committed to the future whereas the final image of the more important pair, Hope and Dalglish, is more tentative.

There are other echoes, visual and verbal, of the earlier film. The saloon, which looks as if Lucia has advised on its décor, has a genuine warmth and gaiety, and there and elsewhere the often mumbled dialogue recalls Altman's way of giving us a feeling of *overheard* conversations. There is, too, no sign of a church. In the new town, Annie tells Dalglish the church is not finished, whereas in the old Westerns it would have been the key signifier of the march of civilisation. In the saloon, and at Lucia's behest, Hope recites, 'There's a grave in old Kirkconnell', and Dillon silences the rowdier elements to listen, and she is followed by Dalglish's easy singing of 'Shenandoah', which establishes him as a crowd-pleaser. The juxtaposition of the two renderings also unobtrusively prefigures an affinity between the two as well as signifying a wider civilisation than the little mining town might be expected to exhibit. There are other such touches: 'Plaisir d'amour' is heard on the soundtrack as Dalglish and Lucia kiss in the brothel, recalling Mrs Miller's music-box version of 'Beautiful dreamer'; Dalglish, who charms everyone, dances with Hope to the strains of Strauss's 'The Artist's Life' at Dillon's wedding; and, perhaps most resonantly, the reciting by the croupier in the saloon, very early in the film, of Shelley's 'Ozymandias'. Both McCabe and Dillon are over-reachers, but in Dillon's case this is allied to a hubristic belief in his own capacity to rule, to judge and to execute judgement. In his doing so, and in the ruin of his ending, the filmmakers could scarcely have chosen a more potent image than that of 'Two vast and trunkless legs of stone', all that remain standing beside a pedestal on which 'these words appear':

> 'My name is Ozymandias, king of kings:
> Look on my works, ye Mighty and Despair!'
> Nothing beside remains. Round the decay
> Of that colossal wreck, boundless and bare
> The lone and level sands stretch far away.'[16]

For 'sands' substitute 'snows' which, if not exactly 'level' in the Sierras, certainly 'stretch far away', with the ruins of Kingdom Come left to scar the whiteness. These words spoken so early in the film prefigure in *their* way the outcome for the man whose past came back to unnerve and unmake him.

A hero of a Western brought to nothing as a result of personal failing (the 'sale', the ensuing autocratic exercise of power) and bad chance is not a common Western protagonist. One thinks of the cattle baron (Spencer Tracy) in Edward Dmytryk's *Broken Lance* (1954), or maybe even more appositely Howard Hawks's *Red River* (1949) in which a cattleman (John Wayne) is supplanted by his foster son (Montgomery Clift), but not many more. This is but one of the ways in which Winterbottom has taken the established genre and refashioned it, just as he has refashioned Hardy's famous novel. He de-romanticises the Western in narrative and thematic elements but in the grandeur and beauty of setting, in the glimpses of a gentler civilisation tenaciously making itself heard and seen, it is as though part of him is still beguiled by the old Hollywood-enshrined verities. In a tantalising if hardly provable comparison, just as Hardy's novels scatter references to classical literatures (*inter alia*, to Genesis, Greek legend, Ariosto, Ovid, the Koran, among others in *The Mayor of Casterbridge*), so Winterbottom's film has echoes of classical Hollywood Westerns. It might well be argued that Winterbottom wears his 'borrowings' more discreetly than Hardy in whom the erudition sometimes seems at odds with the occasion of the reference.

As a Winterbottom film, its generic hybridity is characteristic. *Butterfly Kiss* is love story as well as road movie; *Jude* takes Hardy's tragic tale and invests it with some of the qualities of the road movie; *The Claim* seems enthralled by the central concept of Hardy's novel, but is not overwhelmed by it, as is clear from its daring relocation of the original to make it a Western rather than a Victorian costume drama. In Henchard, now Dillon, Winterbottom has found a protagonist who enlists admiration, apprehension and pity in roughly equal measures and in Peter Mullan he has an actor who can meet its complex demands. His stocky, imposing, grizzled person contrasts with Wes Bentley's younger, softer Dalglish. In fact, it is almost as though the casting choices had been inspired by Hardy's descriptions of the two men. Henchard, when he is first seen at Casterbridge eighteen years after the selling of his wife, is described as 'a man of about forty years of age; of heavy frame, large features and commanding voice; his general build being rather coarse than compact' (p. 37). Dalglish, on the other hand, is depicted in much softer terms, first seen through the girl Elizabeth-Jane's eyes: '[she] saw how his forehead shone where the light caught it, and how nicely his hair was cut, and the sort of velvet-pile or down that was on the skin at the back of his neck, and how his cheek was so truly curved, as to be part of a globe, and how clearly drawn were the lids and lashes which had bent his eyes' (p. 52). Now, that's the girl's perception of him and it is reinforced much later by Lucetta who finds him 'fair, fresh, and slenderly handsome' (p. 188), but Henchard himself later speaks to him of his forehead and nose which remind him of his dead brother, ending with, 'You must be, what – five foot nine, I reckon? I am six foot one and a half out of my shoes' (p. 57). One notes these here, not because Winterbottom has sought look-alike actors, but that he has picked up the essential physical differences between them, differences which are then echoed in their temperaments and behaviour. Both have sex scenes with Lucia, and Bentley, modestly for a Hollywood star, allows himself to be seen appropriately as having much the skinnier torso: the point is that, though Dalglish may be the man of the future, he is in some ways a lesser man, a distinction which is perhaps recognised in his final tribute to the dead Dillon.

There is a great deal more that might be said about this texturally rich film, in its capacities as adaptation, as genre film and as *auteur* production. Western film authority Edward Buscombe's judgement draws attention to the difficulty of pinning it down when he writes: 'Although set against the backdrop of the Californian gold rush, the film isn't perhaps a true Western; ultimately, the violent showdown between Dillon and Dalglish takes second place to the film's domestic drama'.[7] Equally, though, as an adaptation it is far from answering any misplaced criterion of 'fidelity'. It owes its starting-point and overarching trajectory – the spectacular fall of Dillon and the more commonplace rise of Dalglish – to Hardy's invention, but, these apart, it dynamically creates its own world. Both Winterbottom's adaptations of Hardy seem to us exemplary in their approaches, but *The Claim* has espoused a looser relation to its original, whereas *Jude* rigorously scrutinises, sometimes deconstructs, but finally keeps its characters doing what Hardy has them do, where he has them do it.

This study argues that Winterbottom stands to one side of this particular tradition of British cinema, that he has little in common with Merchant Ivory or even *The Wings of the Dove*, that the novels he adapts are raw material which he transmutes into cinematic texts by a rigorous control of the strategies of film. Further, the novels he has so far chosen to adapt do not lend themselves to the decorous habits of the Merchant Ivory film versions of Henry James or E. M. Forster. These films have their undoubted merits, including immaculate production and costume design and uniformly high acting standards, but it is not easy to imagine this team taking on such intransigently austere works as *Jude the Obscure* or *The Mayor of Casterbridge*. It is not that the Winterbottom adaptations of Victorian novels lack these virtues, but that they always seem more seamlessly subsumed in the over-all design and *meaning* of the films. For instance, Mark Tildesley and Ken Kempel's creation of the town of Kingdom Come in *The Claim* is not short on period authenticity; Tildesley is on record as saying, 'We didn't want to fake anything – the drive behind the design was to make it a journey of realism ... We built the town like the new arrivals in the Sierra Nevadas would have built their settlements in the 19th century'.[18] Authenticity mattered, but what emerges goes beyond that to signify not just pioneering hardihood but one man's driving ambition and, in the wonderful pagoda structure that is Dillon's own house, and which is dragged into town for Elena, the film provides the ultimate image of hubris. Similarly, Janty Yates's costume design for *Jude* works unobtrusively and exactly to differentiate Arabella and Sue, while at the same time making apparent their common sensuality. Succinctly put, no one is likely to feel comfortable with these films under the umbrella of 'heritage cinema'. David Thomson's assessment seems truer when he argues that *The Claim* 'deserves to be matched with the great, mad epics of mountains, arrogance, snow and coldness'.[19]

A Cock and Bull Story

After festival exposure in 2005, Winterbottom's eagerly awaited 'version' of Laurence Sterne's *Tristram Shandy* began its general release in the following year, confirming one's sense that the director could not be relied on for a safe, sumptuous Merchant Ivory approach to the literary classics. In fact, anyone even considering Sterne's wildly ludic non-novel for the screen was, *ipso facto*, of a more than usually adventurous, not to say foolhardy, turn of mind. It is a book which stands out as an oddity in English literature, and, published in nine volumes between 1760 and 1767, it can today still astound by its daring. In its self-reflexivity, in its preoccupation with the nature of the novel and its artificialities, it stands as an obvious ancestor to such authors as James Joyce and Virginia Woolf; it has become almost a cliché to describe it as a book that, as Steve Coogan, star of the film, puts it, 'was post-modern before there was any modern to be post- about'.[20]

The novel, narrated by the eponymous Tristram, begins thus: 'I wish either my father or my mother, or indeed both of them, as they were in duty both equally bound to it, had minded what they were about when they begot me'.[21] From the outset, the distinctive voice of the narrator, not actually born until page 199 in the edition in use here, is established as playful, quizzical, idiosyncratic – and it will remain so, until it ends 450 pages later, when this exchange takes place:

> L–d! said my mother, what is all this story about?–
> A Cock and a Bull, said Yorick – And one of the best of its kind,
>   I ever heard. (p. 457)

Tristram's mother might well ask 'what is all this story about?' and Winterbottom has had the wit to use Yorick's reply for the title of his film. Above all, such characterisations point to an author with little or no interest in conventional narrative, and to one utterly beguiled by all kinds of scraps of information, by subsidiary tales, by bizarre circumstances and connections, unable to resist digressions or highly individual approaches to pagination or page arrangement. There are, for example, blank pages, oddities of printing and, on one occasion, a whole chapter is omitted 'and a chasm of ten pages made in the book by it' (p. 219). At first it seemed one had been sold a defective copy.

As to what 'happens' between the quoted opening and closing sentences, the entry in *The Oxford Companion to English Literature* offers the following: 'A sketch of the "story" may be attempted but cannot be very helpful'.[22] In attempting a volume-by-volume account of the work, it gives, for example, this description of Volume IV: 'Volume IV contains Walter's [Tristram's father's] exposition to his bewildered brother Toby of Slawkenbergius's Latin treatise on noses (for which the Shandys are famous), and an account of the misnaming of the infant "Tristram" instead of "Trismegistus"'. A statement such as this about what 'happens' can give no sense of the variety of quirky characters, the rich veins of comedy and pathos, or the range of interests covered in the interminable discussions that ensure that this volume runs for thirty-two short chapters and seventy pages. To read *Tristram Shandy* for 'story' is as improbable an enterprise as it would be to do so for *Moby Dick*, leaving out the 'whaling bits', or *Ulysses*.

What then is a filmmaker with adaptation on his mind to make of all this? Is there a parallel with Harold Pinter's treatment for Karel Reisz's 1981 film version of John Fowles's *The French Lieutenant's Woman*, in which Fowles's reflective discourse on the matter of his 'Victorian' story finds an analogy in the film-within-a-film that provides the structure for the film? It will be interesting to isolate some of the key elements of Sterne's celebrated one-off – the military exploits of Tristram's Uncle Toby and his loyal servant, Corporal Trim, his fascination with fortifications, and his 'courtship' of the widow Wadman – and see what Winterbottom's roguish film has done with them. Less than with most literary adaptations, though, a sense of kinship with the original work is more likely to be achieved not by retention of its 'cardinal functions'[23] but by whether it establishes its own unique tone. Is it, for instance, as interested in the challenges of filmmaking as Sterne is in the processes of his verbal fiction-making? What kinds of equivalents, if any, has Winterbottom sought for such reflections as: 'I enter upon this part of my story in the most pensive and melancholy frame of mind that ever sympathetic breast was touched with. My nerves relax as I tell it. Every line I write, I feel an abatement of the quickness of my pulse, and of that careless alacrity with it, which every day of my life prompts me to say and write a thousand things I should not' (p. 147). Or later, 'I am so impatient to return to my own story, that what remains of young Le Fever's ... shall be told in a very few words in the next chapter' (p. 300).

What in essence Winterbottom and his frequent screenwriter Frank Cottrell Boyce (working together here under the pseudonym of 'Martin Hardy') have done is to have achieved in film terms a correspondence with the novel's insistent playful knowingness about its craft. As the novel plays with the procedures of novel-writing, the film plays with the procedures of filmmaking, both of them having their own underlying seriousness of preoccupation, both of them aware of how formal qualities govern what is 'said'. Just as Sterne's novel offered 'an extended taunt to its audience – promising narrative but endlessly deferring it',[24] so the film toys with the 'events' that make up the narrative of the film of *Tristram Shandy*. As another writer has said, 'What Winterbottom has done is make a film in the spirit of *Tristram Shandy*: a rambling movie about an attempt to film Sterne's novel',[25] though that comment undervalues the structural shrewdnesses of the film. The birth of the titular Tristram is delayed in the film (as in the novel) while father, uncle and doctor discuss modes of childbirth and other matters; the mother, relaxing off-camera, quickly reverts to paroxysms of labour pains; and the grown Tristram discourses to the camera about the boys playing him when young, and apologises to the audience with, 'I'm getting ahead of myself. I'm not yet born'. Lest anyone should think, however, that the film is no more than a grab-bag of knowing self-referentiality, it should be made clear at the start that, just as the relationship of 'affectionate misunderstanding'[26] between Tristram's father Walter and his uncle Toby is central to the novel, so too is the relationship between the characters played in the film by Steve Coogan and Rob Brydon, who play, respectively, Walter, Tristram and an actor called 'Steve Coogan', and Toby and an actor called 'Rob Brydon'. This relationship, in the film and in the film-within-the-film, anchors *A Cock and Bull Story*, not to any kind of neat resolution but to a kind of 'reality' that is witty and uneasy enough to offset mere in-jokiness. Let us look at these two aspects of the film in a little more detail.

There have been plenty of films about filmmaking: as recently as Spike Jonze's *Adaptation* (2003), which begins on the set of Jonze's previous film; the even more eccentric *Being John Malkovich* (2000), and whose writer is having serious problems with his next project; or two decades earlier Reisz's version of *The French Lieutenant's Woman* (1981), in which Fowles's novel is being filmed in Lyme Regis and elsewhere; and earlier still Gene Kelly and Stanley Donen's *Singin' in the Rain* (1952), which makes rather cruel but immensely entertaining fun of silent filmmaking practices. The continental classics, Godard's *Le Mépris* and Fellini's *8 ½* (both 1963), also grapple in narrative terms with the filmmaking process. Reisz's film seems relatively straightforward by comparison with Winterbottom's enterprise. There are some parallels between the modern and the nineteenth-century love stories, and the modern story, involving the making of the film, is screenwriter Harold Pinter's response to Fowles's contemporary commentary on events of a century earlier. Other films such as George Cukor's *A Star Is Born* (1954) and Vincente Minnelli's *The Bad and the Beautiful* (1952) have addressed questions of identity and celebrity, and *Adaptation* confronts the problems of filming 'unfilmable' material, but *A Cock and Bull Story* arguably takes on *all* these and other related issues.

Winterbottom both sharply and affectionately embraces the irritations and excitements of filmmaking as his crew and cast settle into the Norfolk locations chosen for the settings of their film of *Tristram Shandy*. The film starts in the make-up room where Steve Coogan and Rob Brydon are being prepared for their roles, then cuts to Coogan in costume outside the stately home standing in for Shandy Hall, where he tells the cinema audience: 'I'm Tristram Shandy, the main character in this story, and the leading role', picking up on and taking advantage of having the screen to himself to score off Brydon's aspirations to co-star billing. The way the film deals with Sterne's novel not merely mirrors its discursive discontinuities but as well gestures towards what everyone knows about the fragmentary nature of filmmaking: that 'continuity' is a key element in its procedure because almost never is chronological narrative order preserved in the actual filming. And in the inevitable spaces between bursts of filming, there is plenty of time for personnel to stand about chatting desultorily of other things – which, of course, is what Sterne's characters spend most of their time doing. At one point there is a television interviewer (Tony Wilson) talking to his old friend Coogan (who played him in *24 Hour Party People*) about the filming, while the real cinematographer films the fictional cameramen recording their conversation for the fictional DVD. There is a black screen to commemorate the death of a character in a simple semiotic correspondence to Sterne's black page. There are meetings with writer, producer, agent and costume designer; there are gripings about the financial strictures of the filming (in fact, Winterbottom's budget was allegedly cut from £6.5m to £2.8m[27]), with references to underpopulated battle scenes with 'tens' of soldiers acting a crowd. But for all its exposure of the behind-camera wrangling and artifice *A Cock and Bull Story* never becomes just another satire on the film industry. It is pervaded by a warmth for both the book it is – sort of – filming and for the people involved in the process.

If *Tristram Shandy* recalls and diverges wildly from the first-person chronicle that was the characteristic genre and mode of the eighteenth-century English novel, *A Cock and Bull Story* also plays with several recognisable film genres. Its own most obvious genre is that of the film-about-filmmaking, of which there are enough examples to constitute a minor generic category. As well though, it plays – notice how often, without reducing the stature of the work, one uses such words – with several others. The literary adaptation, which of course can cut across other genres, has long been a stalwart of British cinema, perhaps at its zenith in the postwar years of Lean, Reed and Asquith, but resuscitated by the Merchant Ivory team from the late 1970s. The received wisdom was that British filmmakers were more respectful, more 'faithful' in their dealings with literature, which may mean no more than that they were more 'literary' (no particular compliment intended), giving themselves over less expansively to the new medium than their Hollywood counterparts. Mention of Merchant Ivory draws attention to another genre which *A Cock and Bull Story* challenges audaciously: that of the costume drama, at worst made by Merchant Ivory and Sunday night television serials into a parade of brocaded waistcoats adorning actors posed before stately homes. Here, one of the stately homes, Blickling Hall, Norfolk, stands in for the upmarket country-house hotel where the filmmaking crew is holed up. In front of one of the others, Fellbrigg Hall, near Cromer, Coogan/Walter/Tristram confides to us his leading-man status. There is also a continuing discussion about the height of Shandy's heels: while these may be relevant to the notion of authenticity in costume drama, there is concurrently the issue of whether leading man Coogan ought to appear to be taller than Brydon as 'supporting actor' or, as the latter would insist, 'co-star' – 'industrial' matters staking their claim for attention over eighteenth-century 'accuracy'. Another more fleeting genre allusion is to the battle-epic movies, recently exemplified by such nine-figure-budget disasters as *King Arthur* and *Troy* (both 2004): here, the fate of the battle scenes hangs entirely on the dealings with the money men, and the problem is how to make 'tens' of soldiers look dangerous.

One of the most engaging generic influences at work in *A Cock and Bull Story* is that of the documentary – or the mockumentary, or the film-about-the-filming-of, the latter being more usually the preserve of television. Jeremy Northam as Mark, the director, is seen amiably walking round sets between shots, chatting to the cast, dealing with the producer on money matters, standing in for what one knows from interviews about Winterbottom. Northam, as star of *Emma* (1996), *The Winslow Boy* (1999), *An Ideal Husband* (1999) and *The Golden Bowl* (2000), also brings with him resonances of other sorts of filmed costume drama. By 'other sorts' one refers to films which more or less straightforwardly go about the business of rendering accepted classics of page and stage on screen, so that it jolts one to see Northam, usually the well-bred upper-class hero, as the jeans-clad director quietly giving instructions. In a curious way, too, it adds to the sense of documentary authenticity one feels about the whole film: it is a film about a film being made by someone who has had experience in the adapting of such classic costume fiction to the screen. Other documentary echoes are sounded in the 'interview' the bumptious TV journalist conducts with Coogan, and the kinds of chat that go on in the make-up room and costume department and the post-rushes screenings: after all this, it may be difficult to take seriously again those 'making-of' documentaries, more often just lightly disguised promos, that television has accustomed us to.

It isn't only other genres that form part of the film's intertextuality, rich as it is. As well, one is reminded, though not with crudely *auteurist* signifiers, that this is indeed a Winterbottom film. He has filmed literary classics before (see *Jude* and *The Claim*, above) and not been bowed down by the weight of their prestige; he has indeed been willing to subject them to new perspectives, to use them as sources rather than corsets. He has made films with powerful elements of documentary: *Welcome to Sarajevo, In This World, The Road to Guantánamo* and even *24 Hour Party People* are all in part characterised by a tone of low-key this-is-how-it-was filmmaking, that we shake off with some difficulty to remind ourselves that all these films involve re-enactment rather than on-the-spot reportage. One is reminded too of the Winterbottom context by the presence of such cast members as Coogan, Shirley Henderson, Ian Hart and Keiran O'Brien, and of Tony Wilson (of Factory Records fame and thus of *24 Hour Party People*, in which he was played by Coogan) as the interviewer. What with actors playing themselves as well as the characters from the novel (including US star Gillian Anderson as Widow Wadman), we are never allowed to forget that this is a contemporary film, rich in intertextual references, which ensure a persistent pleasure in the post-modernist references that also recall to us how far Sterne was ahead of his time – and on to himself and to his craft as a novelist. Speaking of Anderson and Wadman recalls yet another small and comparatively esoteric intertextual allusion that no one *needs* to know about but which, if one does, injects another echo in the film's already rich texture. In the Victoria and Albert Museum, London, there is a large painting by Charles Robert Leslie (1794–1859), entitled 'My Uncle Toby and the Widow Wadman', first exhibited at the Royal Academy in 1831, and in all likelihood the first visual representation of a moment from Sterne's novel. It is a witty painting in which the widow, clearly knowing what she is about, is 'trying to stir the affections of Captain Shandy'.[28]

The other strand of the film which accounts for most of its pleasure and for its solidity, a solidity that goes beyond mere playfulness however adroit and however film-savvy, is, as suggested above, the relationship between Coogan and Brydon, between 'Coogan' and 'Brydon' and between Walter Shandy and his brother Toby. The film's interest in this set of connections anchors it and ensures that it is *in toto* something more than a jape, however funny it may be *as* a jape, requiring our attention for the affection and exasperation that underpins the dealings of these pairs with each other. A *Sight and Sound* interviewer asked Coogan about his 'competitive relationship with [his] friend and co-star Rob Brydon', wondering, 'Did that ever become uncomfortable?' Coogan's reply was:

> That's what we're like. We do banter like that – I sometimes find it a bit tiresome but Rob wants to do it all the time. We also love each other in the nicest, most untheatrical way possible, but giving vent to the dysfunctional side of our relationship was richer comically and more dynamic

dramatically. It was playing with fire, though – at one point, I really did want to hit him because he was getting very personal.[29]

It is worth quoting that answer in full because it points to the complexities of the interchanges between the two. There is throughout a ripple of unease beneath the professional banter; it has a real edge of mutual rivalry, with its basis in their respective roles in the film-within-the-film but drawing on their extra-textual personas, which here become *intra*-textual as well because they are playing characters called 'Coogan' and 'Brydon' in this film. Both are very well-known in Britain, if less so elsewhere, for their television comedy series, Coogan especially for the inept roving interviewer 'Alan Partridge', in various incarnations since 1994,[30] and Brydon for 'Keith Barret', the divorced Cardiff cab-driver, in the series *Marion and Geoff*,[31] made by Coogan's own company, Baby Cow Productions, which is also involved with *A Cock and Bull Story*. The personas honed in these series, Coogan's self-preening Partridge and Brydon's sad and funny loser as Barret, feed into the kinds of connections the film dramatises. They niggle over billing, with Brydon maintaining that his role as Toby Shandy is really a 'co-lead', certainly 'not a cameo', and the next episode begins with Coogan telling us that his is 'the leading role'. This is followed shortly by a Shandy comparison of Toby's 'groin' wound with the youthful Tristram's accidental circumcision (the result of a falling sash window), with further Coogan complacencies about how, 'Given the family resemblance I felt I should play him [father Walter] as well as myself' – the sort of self-aggrandising comment which needles Brydon. Brydon is not above making bitchy remarks about Coogan (again, their names should always be given here in inverted commas, since they are not the real-life pair, however much they draw on what is publicly known of them): 'Roger Moore is his hero', he tells someone in a put-down about Coogan. And Coogan in turn puts Brydon down when the latter says that 'Originally I was to play Tristram' by riposting, 'Yes, that was when it was going to be a sitcom.'

And so the banter, never wholly friendly but never descending into serious animosity, goes on, involving Brydon's malicious concern for Coogan's declining libido since fatherhood or the recurring competitive sniping about heel size between the two, until the film ends in the rushes room with the two nattering together after the others have left. There is in this moment a warmth of long-standing friendship which convinces us of their capacity to ride out the jealousies and rivalries and which gives ballast to the film's generic hybridity. The Coogan character's relationship with the mother of his child, his partner Jenny (Kelly MacDonald), who has come to the location specifically to have sex with him, is offset by Brydon's snatching the film's biggest international

star, Gillian Anderson, as Toby's love-interest in the Shandy film. And
Coogan's distractedness as Jenny waits for him in bed is an echo of
how Tristram's father's performance there is sabotaged by his obsession with winding the clock. Brydon's anxieties about how he'll be able
to *act* passion with his 'real-life' idol, Anderson, find their echo in the
battle wounds which, she wonders, may have affected his virility. The
parallels with the relationship between the brothers in Sterne's anarchic
novel provide the framework for what may be the most engaging film
ever made about the processes of filmmaking. These parallels throw
up issues of identity, how association with a role affects the capacity to
sift out the real man (does the 'real' Coogan or the 'real' Brydon emerge
here? Could they?) and perhaps alters the nature of that 'real man'. As
one interviewer has said of Coogan in the three roles he plays in the
film, 'he faces the stiffest of challenges, portraying a variation on what
we assume is his real personality'.[32]

It is important to stress the Coogan/Brydon relationship ('a marvel of
acute observation'[33]), and there are other inter-character connections that
might have been mentioned (e.g., production assistant Jennie/Naomie
Harris's crush on Coogan and her rabid cinephilia), in accounting for
how this seemingly ramshackle film is really so firmly and subtly held
together. If this is not just to be a film buff's spot-the-reference treat, it
must have something more universally attractive about it, and this is
located in the director's humorous and humane eye for the foibles and
vanities – and generosities – of the people who are making the film, as
well as for those characters *in* the film they are making. Winterbottom
hasn't notably been a director of comedy: certainly *24 Hour Party People*
has some superbly funny moments, but *With or Without You*, his go at
a romantic comedy, may well be his least satisfactory film to date. In *A
Cock and Bull Story*, though, he has made a film that may well appeal to
those who've never read *Tristram Shandy* (their name is surely legion),
are unfamiliar with Coogan/Partridge or Brydon/Barret, and to whom
notions of intertextuality are inconsequential. On such a level, it can
simply be seen as a very funny film about some more and less compe-
tent people making a film out of a book that seems to be famous for
some reason.

Almost everything about *A Cock and Bull Story* deserves to be
discussed at length and it should be required viewing for anyone going
reverentially about the business of adapting the classics. When one
considers Winterbottom's three adaptations of well-known novels to
date, it is tempting to see him as moving further and further from the
conventions of such filmmaking. *Jude* is a finely intelligent account of
a great bleak literary work, keeping more or less to the main contours

of the antecedent text; *The Claim* radically relocates *The Mayor of Cast-erbridge* both geographically and generically; and now *A Cock and Bull Story* takes an 'unfilmable' novel and makes it the pretext for an investigation of the processes – artistic and industrial – of filmmaking, while over-all providing a commentary on the methods and fixations of Sterne's original.

How does Winterbottom fit into the literary tradition of British filmmaking? 'Literary' means more than merely adapting pre-existing literary works, which he has done; it also connotes certain attitudes to the filmmaking process, such as a reliance on verbal exposition. While it is fascinating to consider these films as adaptations, they may well be more instructively explored as Winterbottom works than as versions of pre-existing texts.

Notes

1 Pierre Berthomieu, '*Jude*: Vivantes couleurs', *Positif*, 430 (December 1996), p. 17.

2 Review of *Jude*, *Cinema Papers*, 113 (December 1996), p. 53.

3 Geoffrey Macnab, '*Jude*', *Sight and Sound* (October 1996), p. 45.

4 Ian Britain, 'Pastoral Images', in Brian McFarlane (ed.), *The Encyclopedia of British Film* (London: Methuen/BFI, Second Edition, 2005), p. 539.

5 Matthew Arnold, 'Thyrsis', *The Portable Matthew Arnold* [1866] (New York: Viking, 1966), p. 158.

6 David Jays, 'Hardier Than Thou', *Sight and Sound* (February 2001), p. 27.

7 Philip Goodhew, 'It Was Grim, I Was Happy', *Sight and Sound* (January 1997), p. 61.

8 Thomas Hardy, *Jude the Obscure* [1895] (London: Macmillan, 1956), p. 82.

9 Macnab, '*Jude*', p. 46.

10 Roger Ebert, *Chicago Sun Times* (1 November 1996), http://rogerebert.suntimes.com/.

11 David Thomson, 'Thomas Hardy in a Cloak of Snow', *New York Times* (7 January 2001).

12 Thomas Hardy, *The Life and Death of the Mayor of Casterbridge* [1886] (London: Macmillan, 1947), p. xxi (future page references to this edition).

13 Roger Eberts, '*The Claim*', *Chicago Sun-Times* (20 April 2001), http://rogerebert.suntimes.com.

14 Will Wright, *Sixguns & Society: A Structural Study of the Western* (Berkeley, Los Angeles and London: University of California Press, 1977), p. 32.

15 Altman has, for instance, revitalised the services comedy-drama (*M.A.S.H*, 1970), the private-eye mystery (*The Long Goodbye*, 1973), the musical (*Nashville*) and the country-house thriller (*Gosford Park*, 2001), as well as the Western.

16 'Ozymandias' (1818), *The Selected Poetry and Prose of Percy Bysshe Shelley* (New York: Random House, Modern College Library, 1951), p. 375.

17 Edward Buscombe, '*The Claim*', *Sight and Sound* (March 2001), p. 45.

18 Mark Tildesley, 'Cruel Intentions', *Sight and Sound* (February 2001), pp. 24, 25.

19 Thomson, 'Thomas Hardy in a Cloak of Snow'.

20 Quoted in '*A Cock and Bull Story*' (21 October 2005), http://film.guardian.uk/london_2005/ (accessed 21 October 2005).

21 Laurence Sterne, *The Life and Opinions of Tristram Shandy, Gentleman* [1760–67] (Ware, Hertfordshire: Wordsworth Classics, 1996). (All further page references are to this edition.)

22 *The Oxford Companion to English Literature*, ed. Margaret Drabble (Oxford: Oxford University Press, 2000), p. 1032.

23 Roland Barthes's term for the hinge-points of narrative. See 'Introduction to the Structural Analysis of Narratives', in *Image-Music-Text*, trans. Stephen Heath (Glasgow: Collins/Fontana, 1977), p. 93.

24 Jonathan Romney, 'The Making of the Unmaking of the Adaptation of the Life and Opinions of Tristram Shandy', *Film Comment* (January–February 2006), p. 33.

25 Sam Wollaston, 'The Life and Opinions of Steve Coogan', *The Guardian* (21 October 2005).

26 Liese Spencer, 'The Postmodernist Always Wings It Twice', *Sight & Sound* (February 2006), p. 16.

27 Romney, 'The Making of the Unmaking of the Adaptation of the Life and Opinions of Tristram Shandy', p. 34.

28 Caption given for the painting in the Victoria and Albert Museum, London.

29 Liese Spencer, 'Steve Coogan: Slightly Less Self-obsessed Jerk, Aha!', *Sight & Sound* (February 2006), p. 16.

30 The original series, '*Knowing Me, Knowing You ... with Alan Partridge*', was first screened by BBC 2 from 16 September to 21 October 1994.

31 First screened in the UK on 26 September 2000.

32 Anwar Brett, '*A Cock and Bull Story*: Slim Shandy', *Film Review* (February 2006), p. 67.

33 Sam Davies, '*A Cock and Bull Story*', *Sight & Sound* (February 2006), p. 48.

1 Christopher Eccleston in the title role, *Jude* (1996)

2 Gina McKee as Nadia in the city at night, *Wonderland* (1999)

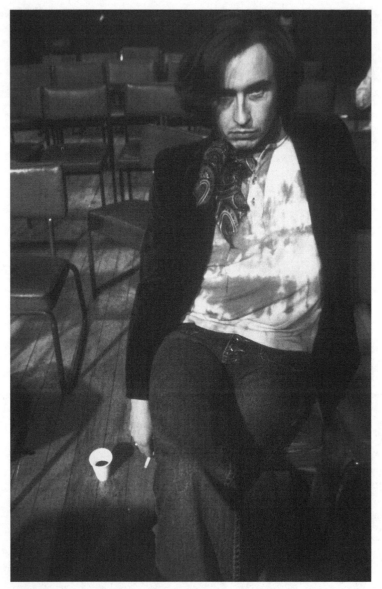

3 Steve Coogan as Mancunian mover and shaker, Tony Wilson, in *24 Hour Party People* (2002)

4 Kingdom Come on the move in *The Claim* (2001)

5 A lighter moment from *In This World* (2003)

6 A grim reminder of what life can be like *In This World* (2003)

7 The director at work. Winterbottom, 2003

8 Rob Brydon and Steve Coogan (as themselves and others) at odds in *A Cock and Bull Story* (2006)

9 Images of oppression in *The Road to Guantánamo* (2006)

Genres reworked

The veteran British director Roy Ward Baker once said when questioned about the range of his films: 'A lot of directors establish a very popular reputation if they specialise, more or less, in one thing', citing Hitchcock's thrillers and Ford's Westerns, and going on to say, 'when I was starting out people used to advise me to make up my mind as to what sort of film I wanted to do and then specialise in it'.[1] In Michael Winterbottom's case, either he has never been given that advice or he has ignored it.

The diversity of his output raises the issue of genre in British filmmaking in unusually vivid terms. He has made literary adaptations strikingly at odds with the prevailing British mode of dealing with classic authors; there is in some of his work a strong sense of the documentary influence at work, when he has been treating subjects of contemporary significance; and there are a road movie, a musical, a science-fiction thriller, a sex drama, and films in the humanist/realist mode. Mere generic diversity would not, of itself, be a matter for critical applause. However, arguably, no other British director, certainly not in recent times, has shown accomplishment over such a genre range. Contemporaries such as Ken Loach, Mike Leigh and Shane Meadows, all undeniably distinguished, are much more easily contained by generic descriptors.

In this chapter we shall consider what Winterbottom has done with such popular genres as the road movie, the musical and the science-fiction thriller, how far he has adapted their conventions to contemporary film practice and ideology, and whether these films, in reworking Hollywood genres, exhibit any peculiarly British inflections. We shall also be concerned with the extent to which he gratifies and/or subverts generic expectations – and, indeed, the whole notion of classical narrative cinema, as defined by the output of the Hollywood studio years in which genre filmmaking became a staple of cinematic entertainment. It will be valuable, perhaps unavoidable, to examine the commingling of several genres in the one film (the road movie crossed with *amour fou* in *Butterfly Kiss*, for instance). It may also be that intertextual references to European filmmakers such as Wim Wenders, Jean-Luc Godard and others, as well as to some US directors, will contribute to the understanding of genre in Winterbottom's films. For, more than most British directors, Winterbottom seems as much a European filmmaker as a British – let alone English – one.

Briefly to draw attention to the concept of genre in film, it is worth quoting Constantine Verevis's recent study, which distinguishes between the semantic and syntactic elements of a film:

> A semantic approach defines a film or genre according to a list of common traits, character types, objects, locations and the like, that comprise the film's iconography. A syntactic approach takes an interest in the various relationships that are established between these semantic elements, the way these are organized in a similar manner to create a narrative structure.[2]

In the orchestration of these elements, genre filmmaking is always drawing on a background of shared recollections about the way films look and sound, how their characters interact in the course of narrative development and how, in relation to the foregoing, they inevitably draw us towards ideological readings, at whatever levels of consciousness on the part of either filmmaker or audience. That last sentence adverts to another characteristic of genre filmmaking: to the cooperation of the audience in recognising the codes at issue in it, over and above the more basic codes required to be read in receiving *any* film, and the audience recognition of such codes constitutes a crucial intertextuality in responding to a film in any particular genre. How far Winterbottom is able to rely on a film-savvy audience in this respect is not of course easy to ascertain. On the one hand, in viewing a film such as *The Claim*, it may be that contemporary audiences are less readily alert to the conventions of the Western than filmgoers of a generation earlier when the Western was an accepted regular on the cinematic menu. On the other hand, younger audiences in the late twentieth/early twenty-first century may well be much more 'educated' about how films work, and will thus make connections with what they 'know' when watching a film that announces itself as belonging to a particular genre.

One simple way of addressing genre as a theoretical concept is to fasten on its twin needs of familiarity and difference: if a film is to be regarded as belonging to a particular genre, it must strike chords of recognition in its audience; if, however, it is not to seem merely formulaic, it must also suggest interventions that differentiate it from the familiar pattern. In other words, it will exhibit the complementary characteristics of repetition and novelty, and it will hope to incite in its viewers the twin responses of recognition and surprise, an acceptable balance between the two working towards an overall gratification. As Thomas Schatz has said in his well-known book on genre, 'the viewer's negotiation of a genre film ... involves weighing the film's variations against the genre's preordained, value-laden narrative system'.[3]

Butterfly Kiss

When *Butterfly Kiss*, Winterbottom's first cinema feature, was released, a year after it was made, it was at once clear that an important new talent had arrived. *Sight and Sound* thought it 'searing', 'a film of numbing power';[4] *Variety* found it, 'An often breathtakingly original meld of road movie, lesbian love story, psychodrama and black comedy', adding that it 'exudes a confidence and distinctive feel that promises something rather special'.[5] The popular magazine, *Empire*, offered a dissentient voice, finding the film generally a 'grimly tedious enterprise'.[6] And when it was finally released in the US a year later still, one reviewer expected that he would 'not see a richer, more moving, more disturbing, or more satisfying film this year'.[7] This bizarre, rigorous, exhilarating, scaring and touching road movie-cum-love story-cum-buddy movie ushered a new voice into British cinema.

The film's very hybridity in genre terms made it something of an oddity in the context of 1990s British cinema. The road movie as such (to use one of the film's favourite qualifiers, as in, 'We only have tapes, not records as such', someone tells Amanda Plummer in the film's first few minutes) is more likely to be American than British. Though the Hope-Crosby-Lamour comedies of the 1940s and 1950s were all called 'Road to ... (Zanzibar, Morocco, Bali, etc), they are not really what one has in mind when one talks of road movies. It may be that the modern idea of the road movie dates back no further than *Easy Rider* (1969) in which two pot-smoking hippies (is that a tautology?) set off across America on motor-cycles. It was imbued with a radical political critique of American conservatism, and may well look very dated now. However, it set a pattern for a modern version of the picaresque, with a subversive approach to conventional concepts of society and sex. Winterbottom himself, in an interview in a French journal, has said that 'c'était plutôt un *road movie* qui nous arrivait via l'Allemagne de Wenders'['it was more like a road movie that came to us via Wenders' Germany'],[8] acknowledging European rather than US generic origins, and perhaps invoking specific titles such as *Kings of the Road* (1976) or *Until the End of the World* (1991).

In 'semantic' terms,[9] *Butterfly Kiss* is easily recognisable as a road movie. Stripped to its narrative bones, the essence of such a film is that it is more or less constantly on the move, and Winterbottom has been an exponent of this kinetic approach in such other dissimilar films as *Jude*, the literary adaptation, and *In This World*, a tale of two Afghan refugees doggedly making their way to London. These three share elements of the road movie in that all three are concerned with a journey on which the protagonists meet both help and hindrance along the way. And, in each case, the journey is always going to be a precarious one. Unlike those in *Jude*, the minatory forces in *Butterfly Kiss* are not those of class and all its constraints; unlike the refugees of *In This World* the protagonists are not fleeing a repressive political regime. Nevertheless, in *Butterfly Kiss* our attention is focused on a couple whose passion and their way of gratifying it places them at odds with their society and pushes them ever onwards.

The road movie that most obviously springs to mind in connection with Winterbottom's film is *Thelma and Louise* (1991), in which the eponymous pair take off for a weekend, leaving some drecky men behind them, meet some more such on the way, engage in murder, and end in a freeze frame that confirms their belief in themselves and their journey. Most road movies till then had involved men, the genre-cross being with the buddy movie as in *Butch Cassidy and the Sundance Kid* (1969), or with a heterosexual couple, as in *Bonnie and Clyde* (1967). But whereas *Thelma and Louise*, directed by British expatriate Ridley Scott, glamorises the women's sexual and other choices, *Butterfly Kiss* does not. Instead of a somewhat soft-centred pandering to a liberal feminist point of view, it is much more hard-headed in its appraisal of what Eunice (Amanda Plummer) and Miriam (Saskia Reeves) get up to. They don't end in mid-air together as Thelma and Louise do – this may now look like a cop-out ending – but the final moments of *Butterfly Kiss*, much less glamorous and star-heavy, and, to be fair, less exhilarating, are unbearably moving. It crosses road movie with *amour fou* and doesn't shirk the *fou* element or the fact that this is not an affair of equals as *Thelma and Louise* was.

In terms of settings and locations, *Butterfly Kiss* offers an iconography at once recognisable as a road movie. This is a world of motorways and service stations and roadside diners staffed by people who aren't finding a great deal of excitement in their workplaces. It is a world in which itinerant characters might be expected. The road stretching ahead, with vehicles thundering past, sets up bleak resonances at some remove from much filming in the British countryside. This is a green but not necessarily pleasant land, but the film doesn't require that we extrapolate from the Eunice–Miriam odyssey to generalise about the state of the nation. To speak 'syntactically' in Verevis's term, the film is organised through a series of 'interviews', perhaps in some kind of correctional institution, where Miriam is talking unreservedly to the camera (it is never specified to whom else) about her runaway relations with Eunice. There is an element of the confessional here but it's more a matter of trying to *explain*, particularly to herself. For instance, in her talk of following Eunice in the first place, she says, 'I suppose it's the worst thing I ever did – but I don't regret it'. Or later, reflecting on Eunice's obsessive behaviour, 'The things she did everyone wants to do'. And most poignantly of all, near the end, 'It's never easy killing someone, is it? Especially if you love 'em'. These black-and-white inserts, acting as punctuation marks in the narrative, do not so much interrupt its head-long movement as give one another view of it – and lead one to see that the central figure is not the mad, driven Eunice but the more ordinary Miriam, whose life is both wrenched out of any course she might have predicted and, whatever its tragic outcome, has been enriched in ways she couldn't have imagined.

Ideologically the film is non-judgemental, at least not in any conventional way. Eunice's obsessiveness, signified initially in the very way she walks, hands in loose blue trouser pockets under long black leather jacket, head down, and then by the dogged enquiries about a particular record in the motorway service station, seems to position her from the start as being outside the bounds of everyday morality. It's hard to imagine a community in which she might have appeared as 'normal'. Kind, dim Miriam, in her sneakers, skirt and padded jacket, breaks out of the little world she inhabits: a world that, as far as we know, is circumscribed by the service station and the council flat she shares with her disabled mother Elsie (Freda Dowie), who says, more presciently than she knows: 'If you don't go out you'll do no evil'. The film doesn't quite encourage us to think it is good for Miriam to be shaken out of this drab little world into a flight that involves a lot of sex and a couple of murders. A feminist reading of the film would no doubt – and rightly – draw attention to the moral unattractiveness of the men they deal with on their way. Equally, though, it wants us to understand why she doesn't regret it.

One would expect that a road movie would have some element of the quest about it that aligns it with one of the oldest western narrative traditions. Otherwise, we shall be left with just a series of events and encounters, both of course crucial to the road movie but requiring for the sake of coherence, of art, some sense of a viewpoint, some shaping agenda. In plot terms, what might have been simple linearity in *Butterfly*

Kiss is broken up by Miriam's black-and-white inserts of address to the camera/to us. And this formal element in the film's construction perhaps connotes in itself a knowingness on Winterbottom's part: our sympathy with Miriam enables us to be appalled by what she does but, curiously, not by *her*. Winterbottom's use of this device obviates the need for any more overt judgement. One doesn't expect road movies to evince the usual signs of rigorous construction that are demanded of, say, classical Hollywood narrative cinema. The film is drawn forward by the lure of the road and derives its tonal coherence from other aspects – from the reckless abandon of Miriam to the lure of heedless, itinerant Eunice. Miriam is overtaken by her awakened sexuality and her love for Eunice with the same inevitability as the road stretches before them. Between them, the beckoning road and Eunice exert on Miriam a pull both erotic and exotic. 'The things she did, everyone wants to do', Miriam confides to us; for her, the secret of Eunice's appeal is that she doesn't just *want* to do things; she *does* them.

There is not space here to analyse in detail all the episodes that go to comprise the film's picaresque plot, but a couple of stages in the film's development need closer inspection, particularly the opening sequences which bring the girls together. After the introductory image of Miriam, pensive, smiling, in monochrome, with Helen Shapiro belting out 'Walkin' Back to Happiness' on the soundtrack, the film cuts to the figure of a girl determinedly walking along a motorway, talking to herself as vehicles thunder past. In the roadside service station, she insists the girl assistant is 'Judith', which the girl denies. Next time we see inside the service station, the assistant's body is lying dead on the floor, her head in a pool of blood. In the next service station, after shots of spiky, muttering, dangerous-looking Eunice tramping along the roadside, she meets Miriam, who is sympathetic to her search for the 'song about love' she's looking for, then goes out on to the concourse and douses herself with petrol to Miriam's agitated dismay. 'I'm a human bomb', she tells Miriam, and, as far as the latter is concerned, so she is, and her effect on Miriam will be explosive. Miriam recognises something exciting in Eunice, and Eunice, who's been expecting to meet Judith there, or so she says, seals their affinity with a kiss, followed by 'Ta'. Nutter at large she may be, but in Plummer's delicately shaded performance she is also engaging and touching: speaking of the non-appearing Judith she says, 'I shoulda known. I don't deserve her'. Her self-effacement here is movingly at odds with the violence of which she has already shown herself capable.

Her explanation to Miriam of the Biblical story of Judith and Holofernes perhaps is oversimplified but its message is unequivocal to Eunice: 'She shagged him in a tent and chopped his head off for the sake of others'. She has her own system of values and lives (and will die) by them, even if these are unlikely to win wide acceptance. After talking incessantly about sex to a truck-driver, she has sex with him in the back of his truck, then kills him. Later, she chats up Robert (Ricky Tomlinson), another lorry-driver, in a roadside café, tries to make him admit he's thinking abut Miriam, teases him lewdly by her (overt) reference to his truck ('I love a man with a big one'), listens outside the truck while he has sex with Miriam, then summarily dispatches him. Their last male encounter is with McDermott (Des McAleer), a travelling rep slightly known to Miriam, at another service station. Talk runs on the lines of 'punishment' (Eunice's body is draped with chains, suggesting she knows of what she speaks), and McDermott engages a double room for the three of them at a motel. 'I love wounds', says Eunice as she licks the incision made for McDermott's kidney operation. When she returns from a shop and finds him having sex with Miriam in the shower, she kills him quickly and they leave in his car.

Singing along with the New Order's version of 'World in Motion' (an apt enough accompaniment), they drive off into the night. This is the song Eunice has been trying to remember early in the film. 'All the time you spent trying to make me good, when all you had to do was turn bad yourself', she chides Miriam, and even at this point a simple 'bad' doesn't seem adequate for either of them. Miriam assures Eunice ('Mi' and 'Eu' as they have now become to each other) that she can do anything Judith would have done. 'Kill me, that's what I really want', is Eunice's reply, and the film moves inexorably to its end. At Eunice's request, Miriam takes her chains off, revealing the wounded body, and they lie together in the lights of the car. Eunice talks of being a sacrificial victim, gives Miriam her leather coat, and they walk through grazing sheep to the sea. 'Now', says Eunice, and Miriam tries to hold her head under. The drowning is shot with tenderness and passion as a pale dawn comes up over the water and 'No Need to Argue (Any More)', performed by The Cranberries, is heard on the soundtrack. Miriam weeps uncontrollably and the film ends, as one reviewer has said, on 'a mythical dimension with this story of two unlikely paired angels of destruction on the road'.[10]

Amanda Plummer, deriding 'This political correctness thing', claimed forcefully that 'the film really has nothing to do with lesbianism. What I got was, "why are you portraying this woman?" ... That it was detrimental to lesbian women to portray them as murderers'.[11] One sees both Plummer's and the feminists' points of view here, but over-all the women's journey is treated with such exuberance, the feeling between them articulated with such generosity and idiosyncratic precision, that the objection quoted seems misplaced. Murderers are presumably no respecters of sexual orientation. It would seem more productive to concentrate on the two superlative performances at the heart of the film, which ensure that it reworks the road movie genre to unusually passionate effect.

24 Hour Party People

'We thought it would be fun to have a lot of music but to avoid people bursting into song', said producer Andrew Eaton. Both he and Winterbottom wanted 'to make a film with great music that wasn't specifically a musical'.[12] In these words, it is made clear that the Revolution team was not likely to be adhering closely to the conventions of the Hollywood musical, even to the sub-category of musicals about professional musicians. These latter are apt to celebrate the rise to fame of the talented, their talents being exhibited via musical numbers which, however much integrated into the film's narrative, have a discrete life of their own. 24 Hour Party People is not like those 'backstage musicals which attempt to pass their numbers off as live entertainment'.[13] The 'numbers' here *are* part of live entertainments which everyone knew about in well-known venues now recorded by the film's cameras (as they were at the time by the newsreels), and the film is as much a study of a time and a place and an enterprise as it is a 'musical'. It is a celebration of popular song[14] as many Hollywood musicals were, but the song being celebrated here is essentially anarchic rather than expressing the utopian vision that was so often at the heart of the musicals of earlier decades. In an essay about the musical entitled 'Entertainment and Utopia', Richard Dyer writes: 'It is important, I think, to stress the cultural and historical specificity of entertainment'.[15] More obviously than most musicals (*Nashville* is another like it that comes to mind), 24 Hour Party People is indeed highly specific about these matters; this is a film about a movement in popular music in Manchester between 1976 and 1992. And as John Mundy suggests, the film 'is a timely reminder that, along with those other structural issues that British cinema needs to engage with, regionality remains important. The city is ever-present ... but it is never sentimentalised'.[16] The film is absolutely centred there, no less so for its notations about how the music reverberated out in all directions, or about what else was going on in Britain at the time (neofascist rallies, garbage-workers' strikes, and so on). The music is aware of the world it operates in but it is also a world of its own.

The film opens with Tony Wilson (Steve Coogan), Granada's regional TV-newscaster, involved in a hang-gliding stunt in the Pennines for his programme, in a filmic trope recalling the New Wave fondness for a shot of the town from the hill beyond. He talks to the camera as he prepares for this stunt: 'This is a physical high – a physical *legal* high – better than sex'. Several earthbound landings later, he admits: 'I'm battered, I'm bruised, I've done something important to my coccyx, I'm slightly upset, and I'm utterly elated'. He has likened himself to Icarus and 'If you don't know who that is it doesn't matter. You probably should read more'. All this happens pre-credits and establishes several important things about Wilson as the film will represent this real-life figure. There's a touch of pretension in the way he talks of Icarus that will echo through his later references to his Cambridge background; he's not without a certain wit, but it is apt to play second fiddle to his self-importance which makes him take himself very seriously. And, formally, he will throughout the film (as Coogan/Tristram will do in *A Cock and Bull Story*) address the camera in a way that contributes to the film's aura of documentary and that both involves and distances the audience from what is going on in the film.

He will sometimes address the audience (that is, us, the camera) while taking part in the on-screen action which he also places at some time in the past. 'I'm a serious fucking journalist at one of the most important times in fucking human history', he tells Granada producer Charles (John Thomson) as they walk through the streets in the immediate post-credits sequence. The film then cuts to the Sex Pistols' famous Manchester gig at the Lesser Free Trade Hall on 4 June 1976, melding 8mm footage of the event with re-enactment. There are forty-two people present as Wilson talks predictively – to us or his TV audience? – while his wife Lindsay (Shirley Henderson), sitting with him in the drab auditorium, looks on, benevolent rather than convinced. The film's time-play is set in motion here: we are watching an event that is meant to have happened perhaps twenty years earlier with comments from someone who was there and, in the film's sequence, is *seen* to be there, but who is addressing the camera and audience as if from a much later vantage point in time.

This concert is the film's narrative take-off point. Not that the narrative has anything like the clarity and causality that classic Hollywood once habituated audiences to, but everything that happens in the rest of *24 Hour Party People* depends from this moment. Wilson is so enthralled by the 'power, energy and magic' of what he hears, that it leads him and his friend Alan Erasmus (Lennie James) to open the Factory Club night to host live gigs by groups such as The Durutti Column and Joy Division. They also release a highly successful EP of the bands that play at the club. His faith in the iconclastic resonance of that first June concert is vindicated and he can tell his TV audience that 'The most exciting bands in the world are coming out of a regional show coming out of Manchester. My show'. So much for Charles's scepticism about the June concert: 'How can it be history if there were only 42 people there?' 'How many were at the Last Supper?' is Wilson's blithe retort.

The plot – the very word suggests something more obviously structured than what happens here – follows the fortunes of the Factory and its Records arm. But this is interspersed with very engaging asides to do with such matters as Wilson's being caught in the back of a van by his wife with his trousers round his ankles ('It's not what it looks', he ventures), while she retaliates with a quick shag in the Factory loo that he unobtrusively interrupts to ask for the car keys. In darker vein, Joy Division is a major success, but it is shattered by the suicide of its lead singer Ian Curtis (Sean Harris), and remakes itself as New Order. Wilson and Erasmus are joined at various points by three other partners – sleeve-designer Peter Saville (Enzo Cilenti), producer Martin Hannett (Andy Serkis) and New Order manager Rob Gretton (Paddy Considine) – and there are predictable differences, but the film doesn't make high drama out of these. The events that follow from this collaboration, including particularly the opening of the Hacienda, are allowed to straggle along with a curiously persuasive verisimilitude. 'Everyone came to the Hacienda. It was our cathedral' and, for a while, 'Manchester was like Renaissance Florence', Wilson tells us in a voice-over as insistent as, albeit tonally different from, that which one used to associate with *film noir* thrillers. The narrative is primarily about the changing fortunes of the enterprises conducted by Wilson and his cohorts and the music is an ever-present accompaniment to this. Wilson's three marriages are presented in the same seemingly unstructured way. He asks Lindsay 'really nicely' not to leave him but she does, and there are subsequent glimpses of second wife Hilary (Helen Schlesinger), whom he visits in hospital, telling us, as he makes his way there, that he's had a child by her, and of number three, Yvette (Kate Magowan), a former Miss UK, 'but that's not what attracted me to her', he assures us unconvincingly.

There is something apparently shambolic in the film's narrative procedures and this led some contemporary reviewers to question its coherence: Philip French wrote: 'The picture, affectionately though not always coherently, traces Wilson's erratic progress ...',[17] and Peter Bradshaw, comparing the film unfavourably to Winterbottom's *Wonderland*, claimed that: 'For all the frenetic activity, this has nothing like the same energy or coherence'.[18] It could be argued, though, that this is a very carefully controlled 'incoherence', intended to mirror the far from clear-cut trajectory of either the Factory and Hacienda's fortunes or of Wilson's private life. Instead, it is a matter of moments plucked out of the recent past by Wilson's not necessarily, or wholly, reliable memory: the opening Sex Pistols concert; the start of the Factory phenomenon with the low-key but very funny meeting between Wilson and Don Tonay; writing the contract for performers in his (Wilson's) own blood; the death of Ian Curtis, following a brief scene of real warmth between him and Lindsay Wilson; the opening of the Hacienda in May 1982 (superbly recreated in Mark Tildesley's production design[19]); the opening of the trendy and expensive Factory office (with its absurd boardroom table); the last night when Wilson invites the clientele to loot the offices and then to leave in a disorderly fashion. The historical sequence of now-legendary punk bands in performance has been placed in a broader historical context, hinted at in, for example, those images of a rally described by Wilson in the words, 'The National Front took to the streets of Manchester today in the biggest demonstration of neo-fascists since the 1930s', or of queues outside petrol stations accompanied by the commentary that 'the strike by the Transport and General Workers' Union is bringing the country to a grinding halt'. It seems that Joy Division's music, particularly Ian Curtis's deranged robot dance, may be a reflection of wider chaos and despair.

Similarly, the other strand of Wilson's life – that of Granada broadcaster for which he wears terrible 1970s suits and ties as compared with the more relaxed apparel he sports at the Hacienda – is a series of moments that don't 'build' in any obvious way but that reveal another sort of life. We watch him, for instance, interview a farmer who has trained a duck to do the work more normally associated with sheepdogs or an old-timer who'd started work on the canals in 1900 ('What do you remember of it back then?' 'Not much.') or his hosting of the TV show, *Wheel of Fortune*, on which he quotes without acknowledgment a street derelict (an uncredited cameo from Christopher Eccleston) on the subject of Boethius and *The Consolation of Philosophy*. The come and go of wives is done with like casualness. Ryan Gilbey's account of *Nashville* uses terms such as 'looseness', 'music-based project' (rather than 'musical') and 'air of informality':[20] these could be applied with comparable appositeness to *24 Hour Party People*. Winterbottom's regular screenwriter Frank Cottrell Boyce claimed to be influenced by Anthony Powell's great novel sequence, *A Dance to the Music of Time* (1951–75) while working on the screenplay, hoping that 'the way [Powell's] characters are picked up and dropped and then re-appear is ... the kind of rhythm you will see in this'.[21] This is an interesting comparison which reflects an approach to narrative that, at the very least, disguises its fictional intentions through use of a first-person narrator on whose memory we rely, and who sometimes casts doubt on his information.

Nevertheless, despite this lack of tight plotting or the usual structural props of causality and careful parallelism or the climactic placing of musical numbers to indicate stages in the genre product, it could be argued that it acquires its own coherence through the centrality of Tony Wilson and of Coogan's performance. Those who are familiar with Coogan's persona as the terminally naff TV reporter Alan Partridge will recognise elements of his self-preening pretension here, but there is more to Wilson than this, and Coogan with very exact, subtle attention to details of manner and inflection, reveals the duality of the man. His TV persona here is not quite as complacent as that of Partridge: the real Tony Wilson was associated with the production (and also appears with Coogan in *A Cock and Bull Story* as an egregious interviewer) and there was surely some concern with what was acceptable to him:[22] he is more likable than Partridge, but takes himself very seriously in a way that precludes our doing so. Several times he refers to his Cambridge background; he is keen on slipping in allusions to 'situationalism' or post-modernism and semiotics, seemingly unaware of how self-promoting he sounds. He is often very funny in this unawareness, as in the moment in which he insists he is right about the first name of the Beatles' Epstein, or when he encourages the TV cameraman to get in a shot of his trendy boots (to reflect his new role as pop-music taste-maker), or *sotto voce* confiding to his crew that they'll have to scrap most of the old bargee's time, or when he's using his on-air time to plug his own musical enterprises. And between these two continuing strands of his life is his fitfully narrated marital history.

Part of the charm of Wilson is in his self-deluding egoism: he can't believe anything is more important than the worlds in which he is involved, whether it is that of 'rave culture' or of his TV shows which he treats with utmost solemnity of intention. The other important aspect of Coogan's role is that of (possibly unreliable) mediator between then and now, between how it was when, as he invokes Wordsworth, 'Bliss was it in that dawn to be alive,/But to be young was very heaven!'[23] and our recognition that it is all past as he talks directly to us, even when present at the actual 'moments'. In this function, his performance is crucial to the film's tonal balancing act as it negotiates its seemingly unstructured way between celebration and a touching awareness that it's all past, refusing the lure of mere nostalgia (it is almost a case of its being *about* nostalgia without *being* nostalgic), between what is comic (his bridling at the suggestion that he has 'huge' hips) and the truly affecting (the Curtis tragedy), utterly eschewing the lure of sentimentality. We may see Wilson as an ungainly fool, willing to exaggerate events and to promote himself as leader of the cultural vanguard, but he remains generally a sympathetic character because of his enthusiasm for eccentric or anarchic cultural forms.

Another balancing act that the film pulls off is that between the seemingly sprawling approach to narrative noted above and the documentary effect it achieves as a result of not engaging in the usual kinds of dramatic strategies. This effect is of course in line with Wilson's own day-job as a news reporter: that from one point of view provides a sort of character justification for the film's procedures. The rise and fall of Factory is, in this film, largely a matter of his narration, or at least as it was perceived by him. As well, of course, the events depicted in the film are essentially representations of real-life events, which tended to happen without elaborate causal interconnectedness. In fact the nearest the film comes to a recognisable 'shape' may be in the metaphor of the 'wheel of fortune', the name of Wilson's TV show: wheels turn and fortunes with them, and this is what happens in the period in which Manchester was the pop music Mecca of the known world – and when it stopped being so. The film in fact mounts a documentary-like argument about the vitality and cultural importance of Manchester at this time, insisting on location-shooting, episodic and elliptical narrative, and on the use of non-actors, as Winterbottom does in several very diverse films.

The making of a film about a history of performances and the deals behind them is echoed in *A Cock and Bull Story* which chronicles the making of a film and the film that is being made: in both there is a lightly worn sense of semi-documentary, of things being done on the run. Further, the film 'subtly blends real newsreel footage with fictional characters so that they all fit convincingly into the same shot'.[24] This formal strategy is not uncommon in Winterbottom's work: others which make use of it include *Welcome to Sarajevo*, *In This World* and *The Road to Guantánamo*. In all of these the blurring of the reality and the re-enactment characterises his approach to known events or, in the case of filming *Tristram Shandy*, of the clearly fictional and what is intended to be viewed as a sort of actuality.

Again, as in *A Cock and Bull Story*, there is in *24 Hour Party People* the phenomenon of actors playing real people, and some of the 'real people' turning up in the film in other guises. For instance, Howard Devoto, founding member of the Buzzcocks, appears briefly as the cleaner who reassures the audience/us after Wilson's sex romp in the panel van: 'I definitely don't remember this happening'; Rowetta, original singer with Happy Mondays, appears as herself; Paul Ryder (bassist with Happy Mondays), played in the film by Paul Popplewell, appears fleetingly; and there are others too. The actors playing the real-life figures were chosen, not necessarily because they looked like the originals, though John Simm does resemble Bernard Sumner, front man for New Order. There is then, as in the later film, an ongoing interplay between the actors and their real-life referents, which removes the film from the usual sense of actors being invisibly accommodated in their roles and their on-screen ambiences. As the *Sight and Sound* reviewer put it, this: 'is a historical re-enactment of a past so recent that many of its participants are still on the circuit, cropping up in genial background cameos (Mark E. Smith, Mani, Clint Boon) or appearing as testy ghosts to take issue with the film's version of events (Devoto)'.[25]

And speaking of 'on the run' above, one of the other unifying aspects of the film is the way in which it literally shows us events on the move. The whole film in fact seems to be linked by sequences in which the characters walk in streets or on mountainsides, or drive about Manchester or tour in buses: it is one of the most incessantly kinetic of films, and when it is anchored in one place, as in the case of the performances, the camera takes over. With the ease of DV filming it captures these concerts from any number of angles. 'With Winterbottom shooting straight, eight-hour days on DV (digital video) – no blocking, no marks, no AD calling "action" – and the accent on improvisation' the actors were given what Coogan has described as 'total freedom to submerge in character and live in the moment'.[26] This intensely kinetic quality is of course utterly characteristic of Winterbottom's narrative style: not for nothing is his first film a road movie or that his adaptation of *Jude* becomes almost another example of the genre, with people kept on the move by their circumstances, as they are again in *In This World* and *The Road to Guantánamo*. His cinematographer in the case of *24 Hour Party People*, Robby Müller, seems to have understood this and has provided a restlessly evocative visual style that captures the moment-to-moment, zestful, undisciplined feel of the Mancunian mythology. Mundy may well be right to say that *24 Hour Party People* suggests 'that, far from being exhausted, the British film musical has a distinct future in its ability to address both the rich heritage of British popular music and its contemporary significance'.[27] Along with Mark Tildesley's production design and the sartorial recreations of Natalie Ward and Stephen Noble (were there ever more grotesque-looking clothes?), Winterbottom has made a film that wryly and wittily and affectionately celebrates a period, a place and a sound without succumbing either to sentimental nostalgia or the put-down of hindsight.

Code 46

If the balancing of the familiar and the innovative is the basic agenda of all popular film genres, and is indeed essential to our learning how to 'read' such films, the matter takes on a new set of meanings when we come to the science-fiction genre. The world depicted needs to have some connection to what we know of our own world – for example, families, dwellings, relationships, work, systems, on the one hand; on the other, we shall expect extensions of such concepts that take us outside our normal range of understandings. As well, we shall expect a film form and style that will accommodate these contrasting expectations. Kim Newman reviewing Michael Winterbottom's s-f piece, *Code 46*, sums up this situation rather well when she writes: 'Film forces more rigour than literature, since spadework that can be dodged by a writer has to be done to show a future world through found locations, set design and advanced but credible technology'.[28] We tend also to expect that a science fiction film will, on another level of meaning, offer some kind of commentary on the contemporary world. In his own words, Winterbottom claimed that 'From the beginning, we wanted to combine elements of the real world in a strange way rather than create an artificial world, to create something that's very familiar and has a lot of texture, but at the same time doesn't quite correspond to anything that really exists'.[29]

This study will be concerned to explore some of the ways in which *Code 46* employs the generic conventions. As with most – all? – of Winterbottom's genre excursions, *Code 46* manages to combine characteristics from several genres. In this respect it recalls how, say, *24 Hour Party People* mates some of the conventions of the musical to a semi-documentary style, or *The Claim* sets us up for a Victorian literary adaptation then transforms it into a Western, or *The Road to Guantánamo* combines political thriller with documentary re-enactment. Certainly on the most obvious levels of narrative events and settings *Code 46* is clearly a work of science fiction, set in some not too distant future. It also bears strong traces of the *film noir* thriller and of the poignantly doomed love story. This latter element has attracted some criticism but it can also be argued that it gives the film a resonance, an after-life in the mind of the engaged viewer, which ensures a greater human significance for the film. In any case, this generic hybridity, so typical of Winterbottom's *oeuvre*, very often makes for a richer texture, a more provocative experience. In the case of the s-f genre, it may be, in any case, that Phil Hardy is right when he says: 'how elusive a genre Science Fiction is', claiming that any attempt at an historical survey of the 'Science Fiction film presents an immediate problem of definition'.[30] He settles finally for the compromise of: 'We are not looking for a pure genre, one that can be distinguished from the thriller or horror in some absolute way, but for those films with significant Science Fiction elements'.[31] Viewed from such an angle, Winterbottom's film is perhaps less exceptional in its approach; what is fascinating about it are, on the one hand, the particular mix of generic and stylistic ingredients it brings to its tale of the future, and, on the other, the kinds of continuity it exhibits in relation to some notable predecessors.

The film begins with a vast overhead pan across a desert tract, over which a set of long explanatory titles about 'Code 46' unfolds. This is arguably a clumsy introduction, alerting the viewer to the possibility that what follows may not be absolutely clear. In fact, some of the narrative details do require very close attention and their significance may not, on first viewing, be wholly apparent, though there is no question of obscurity about the film's main narrative contours. The overhead pan of the bleak landscape proves to be a point-of-view shot: William (Tim Robbins) is looking down from an aeroplane seat and his voice-over says reflectively, 'I think about the day we met'. He is an American investigator, injected with an 'empathy virus', who is being sent from Seattle to Shanghai to discover who has been passing unauthorised 'papelles'. These latter are combined passports, visas and insurance cover, and only privileged persons may have them and, consequently, the right to travel between major metropolitan centres. Those who don't qualify for them are condemned to live in shanty towns outside the cities. The empathy virus enables him to recognise Maria Gonzalez (Samantha Morton) as the leak but, attracted to her, he names another culprit. She introduces William to the friend Damian (David Fahm) for whom she has stolen the papelle. She knows her power over William, they become lovers, and when he returns home and is making love to his wife Sylvie (Jeanne Balibar) he hears Maria's voice talking about 'the consequences of our actions'. In plot terms, it is enough to add that Damian dies of a disease in India, William returns to Shanghai, and finds Maria, all memory of William erased, in a clinic. In love with her, and unable to leave Shanghai because his temporary papelle has expired, he persuades her to secure fakes for them so that they can leave; that is, to commit the very 'crime' he'd initially been sent to investigate. They flee to the port of Jebal'ali, where, after love-making and unknown to him, she reports a Code 46 violation, and they are involved in a car crash. He returns to his wife and child, she is left solitary in the 'outside' wasteland.

'Code 46', as those opening titles have explained, is a product of advanced genetic engineering. As a result of 'IVF, DI embryo splitting and cloning techniques, it is necessary to prevent any accidental or deliberate genetically incestuous reproduction', and 'any pregnancy resulting from 100%, 50% or 25% genetically related parents must be terminated immediately'. Maria has proved to be an exact genetic match for his dead mother – she was cloned from her. So, the doomed love story takes on Oedipal significance: the apparently happily married man, with a stable domestic life back in Seattle, is fatefully attracted to a woman whose genes replicate his mother's. In this mythic allusion, the plot of *Code 46* recalls Jean-Luc Godard's *Alphaville* (1965), in which the 'hero' Lemmy Caution (Eddie Constantine) has fallen in love with a woman, Natacha (Anna Karina), in a far galaxy, has shot her scientist-father, and is escaping with her to Earth, the Outside World, and warns her not to look back. Godard is here meshing the myths of both Oedipus and of Eurydice (and Lot's wife), who was warned not to look back. And the notion of incestuous desire is crucial to the cult Hollywood s-f film, Fred Wilcox's *Forbidden Planet* (1956), a reworking of Shakespeare's *The Tempest*, with the Prospero figure (Walter Pidgeon) clearly harbouring such desires for his daughter.

When one looks at the underpinnings of *Code 46*'s plot, the Oedipal/ incestuous strand is only one, albeit important, element in its texture. What immediately grabs our attention is the 'familiar' narrative paradigm of the man dispatched out of the territory he knows, into an alarmingly strange one, and finally returning to the familiar world. Along the way, he has fallen dangerously in love, been unfaithful to the attractive wife with whom he has had a happily ordered life, then exploited the woman with whom he has become infatuated, finally leaving her to a desolate life while he is restored to the bosom of his family. Winterbottom and his regular screenwriter, Frank Cottrell Boyce, have wrought significant changes on the familiar paradigm. It is considerably less sentimental and banal than Godard's ending in which the fleeing Natacha painfully – and predictably – utters the words: '*Je ... t'... aime*'. *Code 46* articulates a tougher conclusion: Maria's life is irrevocably ruined, partly as a result of her own humanity, partly because of William's intervention in her life, causing her to commit what is for her a crime, and a crime which she is bound to report, while he gets off comparatively lightly. Her final voice-over records: 'I was exiled ... they left me my memory ... they don't care what you think if you're on the outside'. There is real poignancy in the gap between what life has become for each of them separately.

There has been some criticism of what one reviewer described as 'an unfortunate lack of chemistry' between the two leads, so that 'the affair at the heart of the matter remains a passionless business'.[32] This echoed the *Sight and Sound* reviewer who dismissed as 'flatly uninvolving' what she described as 'the rote love affair between bland investigator and pixyish outlaw', though allowing that Robbins and Morton 'try hard to individuate the blanks they are given to play'.[33] There's not much one can do with such opinions except to say that this is not how it appeared to us: that there was genuine intensity and sexy neediness in Morton's waif trapped in the system whose trust she breaches, for the best of reasons, and by which she is finally punished; or that Robbins's apparent 'blandness' seemed appropriate to his role as the functionary of an international surveillance system which discourages personal involvement. Whereas his wife Sylvie stands for the 'normal', in a radically other place he becomes recklessly drawn to a radically 'other' woman. Robbins himself, in an interview about the film, has said about his character at the start of the film: 'I think he's miserable. Imagine that you're the enforcer of a rule you don't believe in any more'.[34] This offers at least a plausible riposte to the idea of his performance as merely 'bland'. Producer Andrew Eaton admitted an element of expedience in the casting of Robbins: they (he and Winterbottom) had cast Samantha Morton, 'and Tim Robbins was very far from being our first choice but he was someone they [the companies involved in financing the production] all liked. So, in the end we had to go with that'.[35] This is only worth mentioning to stress that Bourdieu's 'production field',[36] when applied to film, is a complex of artistic and commercial pressures and motivations.

The love story is at once part of the familiar *and* attached to the strange, the *un*familiar, that is at the heart of the s-f enterprise. So, too, is the film's depiction of the world of great cities that have become so depersonalised that one's life in them is entirely at the mercy of bureaucratic restrictions. There is nothing especially new in that basic scenario in the history of the genre. Think of the workers in Fritz Lang's masterpiece, *Metropolis* (1926), condemned to lives of utterly routine activity, or of Godard's intergalactic automatons at the mercy of the central intelligence of Alpha 60, or the technologised world of *Blade Runner* (1982) in which real feeling has become dangerous and memory can be wiped at will. The cities in which *Code 46* is set are not the product of elaborate production design (the film's budget couldn't run to this) but of actual cities skilfully shot by the brilliant cinematographers Alwin Küchler and Marcel Zyskind. Zyskind, speaking of his experience on the film, says: 'We'd go somewhere that was new and just explore – making the film was a journey'. Of their first stop, Shanghai, he says, 'It's amazing how the city is lit up at night ... Much of the work was about choosing the right place to shoot'.[37] In this respect, the film recalls *Alphaville*, which Raoul Coutard shot in various parts of Paris, and watching this leads one to reflect that nothing seems as *passé* as yesterday's idea of the future. Perhaps, forty years on, *Code 46* will also look old-fashioned in its representation of the city, but, unlike so many of the US would-be epic block-busters of around the turn of the century, it doesn't allow or want us to be overwhelmed by the mindless dazzle of special effects. Writing over twenty years ago of the Hollywood s-f films of that period, Hardy complained that they had 'a degree of escapism at odds with the time that produced them'.[38] Oddly, the magnificent sets for Lang's *Metropolis* now, eighty years later, seem less dated than many of the s-f cities of films made since, maybe because there is a more baroque imagination at work in them. Lang made his accommodation with the familiar in other ways, notably in the oppression of the workers in a brutally capitalistic society.

Winterbottom, in using actual cities and relying on his cinematographers to render them at once familiar and strange, grounds his prognoses in the spread of bureaucratic control from a base we can recognise. Even his use of Seattle is not so far removed from a world we know as to alarm us about how the future might deal with urban life. By concentrating on a world of huge complexes, of internationally kept records relating to everyone's genetic composition, by the use of technologies that seem no longer fantastic but only a decade or less away, by the minimisation of human agency, he forces us bleakly to acknowledge the ways in which our societies have distanced us from a norm of instinctive response to an acceptance of wide-ranging controls. In terms of what is recognisably human, we still have moments of love and friendship, but now they are fraught with perilous possibilities: William's love for Maria ends in exploiting her feeling for him and to her banishment from the scenes of useful living, and her friendship with Damian, the reason for her breaking the rules in the first place, leads to his death. Instead of 'understanding' how another human being may be feeling, William is dosed with an empathy virus that will enable him to intuit accurately without the cerebral effort we may be used to.

There isn't much scope in this deathly serious world for humour, so that the rare touches of wit come over as quite shocking in recalling to us one of the pleasures we take for granted but which may well be lost in this film's predictive view of the world. There's a gently humorous exchange between William and the receptionist at the clinic where Maria has been interned. 'I can tell just by looking at you that you're not just a key-pad presser. You can make judgments', he flatters her. 'Sí', replies this nice laconic woman (Nina Wadia), resignedly trapped in a dreary job. 'And I've just made my judgment about you'. Or there is the airport check-in woman (Archie Panjabi) who turns down his request for a ticket because his papelle has expired: 'What am I gonna do?' he asks exasperated. 'Piss out of the window at 6,000 feet?' 'I wouldn't know enough about your character to say, sir', replies this well-trained official. In these small moments, Boyce's screenplay allows us to see glimpses of a world we know, a world in which 'ordinary' people can surprise us by their grasp of a situation, whatever s-f steps have led to the moment.

'If we had enough information, we could predict the consequences of our actions, but this could stop us from ever making the first move'. These words, spoken by Maria in voice-over and 'heard' by William when he has returned to his wife after his first visit to Shanghai, really encapsulate the main generic strands of the plot. In relation to the love story, if William's empathy virus had enabled him to see the results of his love-making with Maria – an 'incestuously' initiated pregnancy which must be terminated; his later use of her special access to official records to fake a papelle; her need to report herself and her subsequent exile – it is just possible he might not have made 'the first move'. But the film leaves such a question open-ended. With enough information to enable accurate prediction, he might still have sought to gratify his own infatuation. As to the basic s-f plot, a full knowledge of the strictures of Code 46 might well, and no doubt properly, have inhibited the taking of a first move that will result in incest and criminal violation. And knowing about the local disease to which Damian succumbs in India might well have predisposed Maria not to have provided him with the papelle he needed to get there. Regarding the *film noir* mystery strand, William, with full information of any of the outcomes referred to in the preceding sentences, would surely not have allowed his attraction to Maria to compromise his official role in being sent to Shanghai.

Just as director and screenwriter have achieved a taut coherence through this thematic knot-tying, so too Winterbottom has orchestrated the various other contributions to the over-all patina of his first excursion into the s-f genre. The production design and cinematography collude to produce myriad superb cityscapes, which are as impressive in their way as the constructed cities of such renowned predecessors as *Metropolis* or *Things to Come* (1933) or the part-studio, part-location settings for *Blade Runner*. Some interiors were shot in London studios, but *Code 46* is mainly location-filmed, which is Winterbottom's stated preference:

> Most of my films are observational in some way, so without a sense of place, and how the characters are going to react to each other in that space, it's hard for me to tell who the characters are going to be. So to build a completely artificial futuristic world on studio sets would not have worked for me or for the film.[39]

There are various accounts of how, locations having been scouted in advance, the shoot proceeded efficiently and quickly, using available light as far as possible and, in the case of production designer Mark Tildesley, melding material from several locations to give a sense of strangeness but never engaging in a sort of interior design that would distract from the central story. Producer Andrew Eaton had this to say about the film's 'look':

> To make a science-fiction film set in the future you either go to Shepperton and spend millions of pounds making a big set or as in this case we decided to go to existing places that had really unusual architecture and a different mix of culture.[40]

No doubt, as suggested elsewhere, Winterbottom's having surrounded himself with such regular collaborators as Eaton, Tildesley, Cottrell Boyce, Zyskind, Küchler, editor Peter Christelis and costume designer Natalie Ward helps to account for his prolificacy, especially given his predilection for filming in demanding locations. In the case of *Code 46* these talents have combined to recreate a world that at once echoes disturbing elements of the one we know and, uncomfortably, suggests extension of these in a not-too-distant future. Eaton, talking about the film's genesis, said:

> One of the ideas for that film came out of our experiences of working on *In This World*, the whole bureaucratic, diplomatic challenge of getting visas for people and going into these different countries was a real eye-opener to us. It seemed to us that a lot of that was already happening, it wasn't much of an extension.[41]

One of the recurring characteristics of the s-f film is its prognostic agenda. It is perhaps not going too far to say that this agenda includes a minatory overtone, a warning that, if the world does not pay heed to certain signs discernible in contemporary society, then the future may be at risk as far as, say, freedoms we take for granted are concerned. Alienation in an increasingly technology-dominated world has been a theme in such films at least since *Metropolis*, in which one of the most striking images is that of the workers in a massed queue to start the shift in their underground workplace, replacing an equally vast, undifferentiated queue moving in the opposite direction as *its* shift finishes. *Things to Come*, derived from H. G. Wells's didactic novel, imagines the world in 2036 as a technological Utopia, but against which humanist impulses finally rebel. The intergalactic world of *Alphaville* has reduced its inhabitants to mutants forbidden the very words of 'love' or 'conscience', let alone the concepts. In Kubrick's *2001: A Space Odyssey* (1968), the central intelligence is housed in a computer called HAL: audiences had then

just enough inkling of the scope of computers to respond to this technological protagonist, and by the 1990s every child of three would be quite
at home in front of a computer screen. By the time of *Blade Runner*, our
apprehensions of urban decay were already disquieting enough for us
not to feel too great a strain in accepting its vision of Los Angeles in
2019. And so on. All these films, like *Code 46*, 'call into question the
world we live in and accept as absolute', Hardy says, going on to claim
that 'of all the film genres, Science Fiction is the most revealing of the
times that produced it'.[42] Though usually set in the future, its real tense
is the present and its real subject is the anxieties of that present and how
these might manifest themselves in the actualities of the future.

One of these recurring anxieties seems to be that, whatever the technological advances the world can anticipate in the foreseeable future,
there is no guarantee of the increase of human happiness. Quite the
contrary, in fact. Like most of those films mentioned in comparison
with *Code 46*, there is a troubling tendency towards ever-greater bina-
rism in human society. As far back as *Metropolis*, there is an alarming
divide between the sybaritic luxury of the life-style of those in control
and the relentless oppressiveness of the workers who live in a real and
metaphoric underground hell. The supposed Utopia of *Things to Come*
founders on the chasm between the pompous, complacent rulers and
those who stand for humane values. Those who live in *Alphaville* know
that there is a World Outside, which they will never enter and are indeed
forbidden to speak of. And in *Blade Runner* there is a stark contrast
between those who live in the luxury of the Tyrell building and those
who just survive in the squalor of the streets. In *Code 46*, those who
are deemed to be sufficiently productive and useful live in the closely
guarded metropolitan centres while those with less to contribute are
condemned to the Outside, a series of desert wastelands, perhaps
showing the effects of climate change. Those Outside have no hope of
re-entry to the privileged sites of the cities, though in truth these are in
their own way uninviting.

Code 46 may lack the grandeur of concept of some of the famous titles
invoked here by way of comparison, but in its non-didactic and unpor-
tentous way it is as riveting and unsettling as some of the more famous
exemplars of the genre. It explores a system whose cruelty condemns
some – finally, Maria – to life Outside and there is real poignancy in her
final voice-over as she sits solitary with her back to the camera, 'They
left me my memory. They don't care what you think if you're on the
Outside'. The film has had only very modest box-office success, and it
may be that its vision is too bleak and that its view of how things are now
is too troubling to attract the crowds that prefer an upbeat gesture at the

end. Instead of the special effects crucial to multiplex hitdom, this is a science-fiction film with brains.

Conclusion

Michael Winterbottom is hardly a genre director as the term is usually understood. Rather, he is a filmmaker who ventures into the territories occupied by a range of genres and rarely leaves them as he found them. His road movie (*Butterfly Kiss*), despite its European affiliations (e.g., with the French *Baise-Moi*, 2000) and his musical (*24 Hour Party People*), despite recalling *Nashville*, are distinctly British in tone. This is not just a matter of setting but of a smaller-scale, more humanly focused approach to the respective categories. His science-fiction film is not as wild (one is happy to say) as *The Matrix*, for instance, but is persistently more thoughtful, interested in what might happen to humanity.

Notes

1 Roy Ward Baker, interview with Brian McFarlane (London 1990).
2 Constantine Verevis, *Film Remakes* (Edinburgh: Edinburgh University Press, 2006), p. 84.
3 Thomas Schatz, *Hollywood Genres* (New York: Random House, 1981), p. 10.
4 Lizzie Francke, '*Butterfly Kiss*', *Sight and Sound* (August 1995), p. 42.
5 Derek Elley, '*Butterfly Kiss*', *Variety* (February 20–26, 1995), p. 73.
6 Clark Collis, '*Butterfly Kiss*', *Empire* (September 1995), p. 42.
7 Rocco Simonelli, '*Butterfly Kiss*', *Films in Review* (May–June 1996), p. 68.
8 Michel Ciment and Yann Tobin, 'Entretien avec Michael Winterbottom', *Positif*, 430 (December 1996), p. 25.
9 See Verevis, *Film Remakes*.
10 Francke, '*Butterfly Kiss*'.
11 Interview with Rocco Simonelli, *Films in Review* (August–September 1996), p. 79.
12 FAC401, *24 Hour Party People*, Production Notes, p. 6.
13 Jane Feuer, *The Hollywood Musical* (London and Basingstoke: Macmillan Press/ BFI, 1982), p. 45.
14 Feuer's Chapter 3 is called 'The Celebration of Popular Song'.
15 Richard Dyer, 'Entertainment and Utopia', in Rick Altman (ed.), *Genre: The Musical* (London and New York: Routledge & Kegan Paul/BFI, 1981), p. 176.
16 John Mundy, *The British Musical Film* (Manchester: Manchester University Press, 2007), p. 254.
17 Philip French, 'The Mancunian Candidate', *The Observer* (7 April 2002).
18 Peter Bradshaw, '*24 Hour Party People*', *The Guardian* (5 April 2002).
19 Tildesley, said: 'Initially I was hoping that we could use the original building. When I was brought on board, the actual Haçienda was still in place, it had been sold to a property developer and though we tried some early negotiations about keeping the place alive until such time as we could finish filming, as ever with

developers, that crumbled into nothing' (in the film's Press Kit, p. 11).

20 Ryan Gilbey, *It Don't Worry Me: Nashville, Jaws, Star Wars and Beyond* (London: Faber and Faber, 2003), pp. 127, 128.

21 Quoted in FAC401, p. 7.

22 The film's website contains interview material with a number of the cast who comment on the difficulties of playing real people who were still alive and around the set in some cases.

23 William Wordsworth, *The Prelude* (1799–1805), Book xi, ll, 108–9, *Longer Poems* (London: J. M. Dent & Sons Ltd, 1946), p. 379.

24 Roger Ebert, 'Pranksters: *24 Hour Party People*', *Chicago Sunday Times* (16 August 2002).

25 Xan Brooks, '*24 Hour Party People*', *Sight and Sound* (May 2002), p. 55.

26 Colin Kennedy, 'Sex+Drugs+PunkxAcid', *Empire* (May 2002), p. 83.

27 Mundy, *British Musical Film*, p. 254.

28 Kim Newman, '*Code 46*', *Sight & Sound* (October 2004), p. 49.

29 Quoted in Davis, '*A World Apart*', p. 57

30 Phil Hardy, 'The Science Fiction Film in Perspective', in Hardy (ed.) *The Aurum Film Encyclopedia: Science Fiction* (London: Aurum Press, 1984), p. ix.

31 *Ibid.*, p. xi.

32 Tom Ryan, 'Movies', *The Sunday Age*, Melbourne (5 June 2005), Preview, p. 14.

33 Newman, '*Code 46*', p. 49.

34 Tim Robbins, 'The Drugs Don't Work', *Starburst* (March 2005), p. 52.

35 Interview with Brian McFarlane (London 2006).

36 Pierre Bourdieu, *The Field of Cultural Production* (ed. and trans. Randal Johnson) (Cambridge: Polity Press, 1993). See Part I, Chapters 1–3.

37 Quoted in Davis, '*A World Apart*', pp. 57, 58.

38 Hardy, 'The Science Fiction Film', p. xv.

39 Winterbottom in Production Notes for *Code 46*, Becker Entertainment, p. 5.

40 Andrew Eaton, interview (May 2006).

41 *Ibid.*

42 Hardy, 'The Science Fiction Film', p. xii.

6

Melodrama, sex, beaches and other interests

While one of the distinguishing characteristics of Winterbottom's *oeuvre* is his way of taking recognised genres and treating them in idiosyncratic ways, some of his work defies easy categorisation. A film such as *Go Now*, made for television but shown in cinemas in some countries, is a case in point: it exhibits some of the informing traits of melodrama but its treatment is in certain essentials realistic, avoiding the gratifications of melodrama, at least as the mode is practised in Hollywood cinema. Again, *With or Without You* raises expectations of romantic comedy but deflects – or dissipates – these with a surprising acridity of tone; and the *noir*-influenced *I Want You* hovers between thriller and erotic drama. And how does one designate *9 Songs*? Realist sex and concert scenes, to the point where there is almost a whiff of documentary in the film's short footage, but it also has a vestigial narrative continuity. Generic hybridity is no barrier to aesthetic achievement, but apart from *Go Now*, where it is more a matter of tonal complexity than genre mix, these films are among Winterbottom's least successful.

Go Now

Winterbottom's regular producer Andrew Eaton, co-founder of Revolution Films, has said: 'I've never quite understood why people have made such a distinction between the two mediums. I think it's about ambition and vision and what you think you're trying to make'.[1] These words are relevant to one's view of *Go Now*, originally made by Revolution for BBC television, but quite widely shown in cinemas, especially in the US. Watching it on the DVD version admittedly, one is reluctant to label it with the put-down term, 'telemovie'. There was a time when there seemed to be a sub-genre that might have been cynically written off as 'disease-of-the-week' films especially made for television, like Fielder

Cook's *A Love Affair: The Eleanor and Lou Gehrig Story* (1978) or John Erman's *An Early Frost* (1985) or *The Last Best Year* (1990). In fact the cinema itself has a long history of films about people suffering from serious illnesses, more often than not featuring beautiful actresses, such as Margaret Sullavan in *No Sad Songs for Me* (1950) or Ali McGraw in *Love Story* (1970) or Debra Winger in *Shadowlands* (1993), on whom the progress of the disease makes little observable impact.

In the sort of context provided by titles such as these, *Go Now* looks distinctly realistic, so that the following comment of one critic seems unduly severe: 'For the most part, *Go Now* conforms to the standards of television drama. This is manifested in both the popular TV-movie theme of learning to live with serious illness and in the dominantly conservative visual style'.[2] To a very considerable degree, it avoids the clichés of its kind, above all the sentimentality so often endemic in such tales of suffering and the eschewing of the realities of the progress of the disease. In Winterbottom's *oeuvre*, *Go Now* may be seen to draw on his television work, including his highly regarded, BAFTA-nominated *Family*, and to anticipate his prolific cinema output, poised as it is almost between the two and just after his first clear cinema film, *Butterfly Kiss*. As Eaton said of making *Family*: 'When we were doing *Family* we still thought we were making a *film*. It had to be split into four story parts and we edited a two-hour version of that and it was shown at some film festivals'.[3] His point was that he and Winterbottom made no clear distinction between the two media, and it is worth keeping this in mind when considering *Go Now*. In some ways, it is tighter in scope than some of the feature films: it deals with a small group of people in one town rather than invoking the geographic sprawl of such later films as *Welcome to Sarajevo* or *The Claim*; its interests are intensely personal, not overtly political as in films such as *In This World* or *The Road to Guantánamo*; it is an original story, not adapted from a well-known novel as *Jude* or *A Cock and Bull Story* were; it doesn't try to embrace the multiple narrative strands of, say, *Wonderland*. If the 'made-for-television' descriptor implies focus on a single story-line, then, yes, one sees that *Go Now* has such affiliations; if, though, it implies that the film lacks passion and resonance beyond that single story-line, then, no, it is as much a *film* as anything else Winterbottom has done.

The film's narrative shape is rigorous and, indeed, almost classically straightforward as it moves from starting situation, through complication and reactions to this, and to resolution. Its protagonists are plasterer Nick Conran (Robert Carlyle), a soccer player who is having an off season, and Karen (Juliet Aubrey), who works as a hotel administrator. They meet at a pub where Nick rescues her from the unwanted gropings of her dance partner, and, after several sexual and other encounters, she moves in with him. The love story (a feebly sentimental term for what it will prove to be) is established, before the crisis of Nick's illness, its commitment contrasted with the serial womanising of Nick's friend Tony (James Nesbitt), who fancies Karen's former roommate, Paula (Sophie Okonedo). After a couple of incidents at work, some blurring of vision in the street and an accident when driving, Nick is confirmed as suffering from what may be multiple sclerosis.

This provides the crisis for the narrative. Nick's rowdy football mates hardly know how to behave with him, enraged as he is at the least sign of patronage, but the film really pivots on his relationship with Karen. He becomes increasingly difficult to live with: Paula warns Karen that she's 'throwing her life away'; and Karen herself, admitting that they're just 'living together' with no thoughts of 'marriage or kids or anything', is also aware that she *has* a choice. It's more clear-cut for Nick: he 'has to get on with it'; she *could* leave him. From this point the film moves to its most powerful scene, in which Nick tells her to go, accusing her of 'taking charge', while she suspects his bitterness is his way of releasing her. She stands outside his house in the rain, refusing to leave, in spite of his saying, 'If you don't go, I'll kill myself', and, via a vertiginous 360-degree shot, he finally moves towards her – and towards the film's denouement. There will be no reprieve for him and it will be difficult for her, much as she says, and might like to believe, that 'Nothing's changed'. The film ends on their wedding day, but not by way of shirking or even minimising the challenges that must inevitably lie ahead.

One of the film's most interesting qualities is the way in which it draws on characteristics of, and refuses categorising as either, realism and melodrama. Recalling our earlier reference to Verevis's useful discrimination between 'semantic and syntactic elements'[4] in his discussion of genres, it is helpful to invoke it again here. Though realism and melodrama may be considered as modes rather than genres, the semantic/syntactic distinction points to how a tonal complexity works in *Go Now*. In semantic terms and in relation to realism, place is observed in punctilious detail, whether the location is the pub, the flats in which Nick and Karen live, the football clubrooms and locker room, hospitals, and so on. The treatment of the city in fact recalls those British New Wave films, such as *Saturday Night and Sunday Morning*, with their loving regard for street scenes, for distant prospects and noisy interiors. Though the city is not named (as Belfast will be in *With or Without You*), Winterbottom makes valuable use of his Bristol locations. It was a city he knew, as he had studied film at Bristol University: 'Je connaissais bien ce quartier très particulier de Bristol', he told an interviewer, finding in it 'un mélange social très intéressant' ['I knew this part of Bristol well ... a very interesting social mix'].[5] There is, for instance, a striking shot across the docks looking towards the Cathedral.[6] Nick and Karen wander along Royal York Terrace, Bristol's most famous Georgian Street, in Clifton, and several times (exhilarating on one occasion, arduous later as the illness progresses) they run across Isambard Kingdom Brunel's Clifton Suspension Bridge, over the Avon Gorge. They meet his parents at Temple Meads Station (another Brunel landmark); wander about St Nicholas Market, in the old part of Central Bristol; and go for a drink in another old part of the City (probably King Street), which has a cobbled surface. Without specifying the place by name, Winterbottom, in choosing readily identifiable locations, has insisted on the specificity of place. As in so much of his work, place is more than background or an excuse for pictorialism; it is registered as a key factor in the lives of the characters, though without perhaps the polemical intention of the New Wave films.

The range of character types – workmen, footballers, girlfriends, parents, doctors – is essentially realist in its orientation: there is no suggestion of characters who might more properly belong in a different sort of convention. As well, to take a syntactic approach, one finds a strongly realist aesthetic at work in the careful, non-sensationalist charting of the progress of the disease: it is dramatised in small incidents from which a cluster of symptoms emerge, rather than a 'big scene' in which the diagnosis is spelt out. And up to a point, the way the central relationship is seen to develop from sexual gratification to something deeper and the emotional dealings with the illness are also presented with a concern for realist detail. Consider, for example, the scene in which Nick's parents, who have come to stay with him and Karen, listen to the account of the progress of the disease: the feelings flowing round the kitchen table here are quietly rendered in dialogue and mise-en-scène. A French critic, writing on the film's tonal/generic complexity, has noted how 'Go Now réunit ainsi plusieurs composantes propres au mélodrame' but that, in the manner of Ken Loach, 'Winterbottom fait ici oeuvre sociale en mettant en lumière la vulnérabilité de l'ouvrier, simple détenteur de sa force de travail, face au système social. ['Go Now thus combines several strands characteristic of melodrama' but that, in the manner of Ken Loach, 'Winterbottom is making a social contribution by highlighting the vulnerability of the worker, the simple possessor of the power to work, face to face with the social system'].[7]

However, though the film does in some ways echo those early 1960s forays into British northern realism, in matters of both semantic and syntactic significance, it also, to its own advantage, draws strongly on some of the conventions of melodrama in the way it, to paraphrase Vere-vis's words, organises the relationships between its semantic elements. The narrative pattern of classical Hollywood melodrama involves such key elements as an over-all pattern set up by a goal or enigma or desire, which gives shape and purpose to the whole enterprise, and which is articulated through a series of causally connected events that constitute the plot. The establishing of this cause-and-effect chain is marked by a powerful use of parallelism, sometimes for comparison, sometimes for contrast, but always moving the narrative towards a strong sense of closure. Some of the kinds of connection suggested in this brutally truncated account are exhibited in the narrative practice at work in *Go Now*. There are, for instance, strongly felt oppositions between the lad culture to which Nick has belonged and the access of other sorts of sensitivity in his burgeoning relationship with Karen, between the intense physicalities of either the football or sexually charged scenes, on the one hand, and the incapacitation that ensues from Nick's disease, on the other. The over-arching pattern of the plot may have the final wedding scene in its sights from the outset, but, in the ways to which Hollywood melodrama has accustomed us, this resolution is blocked by conflicts and obstacles that delay its satisfaction. The film *does* make its way to a gratifying if muted closure, but does so through no sacrifice of its integrity, and this may well be the result of the realist underpinning of the melodramatic structure.

The foregoing is not to make heavy weather of one of Winterbot-tom's earlier and lesser films but rather to draw attention to the kind of hybridity, whether of mode or genre, that makes some of his work difficult to classify. The film's visual and editing styles reinforce one's sense of *Go Now*'s being – to repeat Eaton's words about 'ambition' and 'vision' – as much 'film' as anything else he would eventually do. Even so early in his career Winterbottom was willing to take stylistic risks, as in the way he disrupts realist expectations with the sudden insert of black-and-white freeze frames. These have the effect of snapshots, in which the football ambience and its gross, anything-for-a-laugh culture is captured, with joky captions. In one set of such shots, Tony drops his shorts on the field and turns towards the umpire so as to 'give him some cheek'; in another, when Nick is first in hospital with his hand in plaster, the caption reads: 'Nick makes a last attempt to stop wanking'. We are meant to interpret these, not as wit, but as what passes for it in this laddish culture. The jokes are later critiqued for the schoolboy smut they basically are when Nick is no longer able to respond to locker-room banter about erectile difficulties, but the continued contrast between this culture and the reality of Nick's experience is one of the means by which sentimentality is kept at bay. Another is in the way the film's tempo is stepped up, from the longish scenes in which the early part of the narrative is developed through the increasingly tense, brief segments of the second half of the film, acting out the unpredictable processes of the disease, and then easing into the last sequence of the wedding. This latter is a triumph of tone: the temptation to glutinous sentiment must have been strong, but the final moment when Karen helps Nick to his feet on the dance-floor has been so carefully led into (by Nick's father's dancing with Karen while his mother takes up an unobtrusive stand behind his wheelchair; by footballer Del being sick in the toilet, having 'found that the bar is free'), that the effect is both optimistic and heart-breaking, but not tear-jerking. The *Variety* reviewer was right to praise the way the film 'maintains its energy, non-maudlin tone and high quotient of dry humour'[8] until the end.

Whatever its mix of modes, the abiding impression one takes of the film is that of its humane concerns for these lives. Whether it is a matter of a smartly edited montage that acts out aspects of Nick and Karen's life together in the flat, including his doing plaster repairs (recalling his trade) or the great extended penultimate sequence in which she stands determined in the rain as he observes her from his upper-floor window, and the stages through which they arrive at the embrace of commitment, Winterbottom reveals not only his early mastery of film narrative technique but, as well, the compassion for lives under threat which has been so central to his work. Think of the doomed young women in *Butterfly Kiss*, of Jude, of the lives ripped apart in *Welcome to Sarajevo*, the refugees in *In This World*. One admires him for his stylistic venturesomeness, but perhaps even more as a modern exemplar of the screen's humanist tradition. In *Go Now*, he has the advantage of beautifully exact performances from Carlyle and Aubrey (one of British cinema's best and most under-used actresses), supported by the contrasting pair played by Nesbitt and Okonedo and the touching minimalism of Tom Watson and Barbara Rafferty as Nick's parents, in their turn contrasted with the raucous lads of the soccer side.

Go Now is prentice work by comparison with some of the more daunting projects Winterbottom has undertaken, but its excellences are not only admirable in themselves but offer proleptic hints of the major work he would go on to do.

I Want You

This is one of Winterbottom's most curious, most unsettling films – and one of the least seen. It is, however, a very assured piece of film-making, and perhaps its failure to find substantial audiences is the result of its marriage of several modes which leave the viewer somewhat stranded. Like *Go Now*, its narrative has strongly melodramatic tendencies, leading here to a tragic turn of events rather than to the tentatively upbeat closure of *Go Now*, which it also resembles in its use of realist trappings in matters of location and of the minutiae of daily lives. But it is also essentially a mood piece rather than a riveting narrative, and this mood is achieved through its pervasive overlay of *film noir* stylistics. The *Variety* reviewer is probably right in summarising its impact as 'an ambitious idea that succeeds more as a stylistic exercise than as an involving, fully realized drama'.[9]

Its central figure is Helen (Rachel Weisz), who runs a hairdressing salon in a south-coast town called Farhaven (actually shot in Hastings and Dungeness). Assured, capable, sexually confident, she is the focus for the attentions of three males: the mute Yugoslavian teenage refugee, Honda (Luka Petrusic), whom she meets by accident, literally, when she knocks him over as she rides her bike along a beach-side pavement, in the film's most arbitrary instance of intersecting lives; Bob (Ben Daniels), the local DJ, whom she has been stringing along for some months; and Martin (Alessandro Nivola), who has returned to the town after nine years away – in gaol. Honda establishes a connection with her when he returns the bracelet she has dropped in their collision, and pays her innocent tribute with flowers. By contrast, she refuses to accept Martin's flowers; she refuses to let Bob make love to her, and he is enraged when he finds that Honda has managed to record her aborted session with Bob in his car.

The narrative will discard Bob fairly perfunctorily: he is clearly a hypocrite as the film contrasts his high-minded moral approach on air with his predatory pursuit of Helen. In the film's thematic patterning, he may be seen as representing another kind of defective communication, when he encourages women to phone in instances of assault while ready to practice it (against both Helen and Honda). Honda's muteness has led him to obsess with the need to record and listen to kinds of (sexual) life in which he can play no part, except that of voyeur or adoring admirer; and Martin's telephone calls to Helen, as he tries to re-establish contact with her, fail as she listens but will not reply. Helen's sexual power is the pivot on which the narrative turns: she is willing to tease a man she meets at the pier dance-hall; she also teases Honda, running her bare toes over his leg and thigh. She is being established as a *noir* protagonist: in Weisz's performance, she is sensually attractive and, though early presented as a victim, is then seen to constitute a danger to the men she comes in contact with.

The film begins with a voice-over (we later realise it belongs to Honda's sister, Smokey) saying: 'I imagine it happened something like this, but I don't know for sure. It all happened a long time ago, years before I came to Farhaven'. A body in a bag is dropped into water; the voice-over continues: 'It was the end of one story and the beginning of another'. The credits then appear, and are followed by a cryptic scene in a bedroom where a woman sleeps and a man packs a bag and leaves. The film then cuts to Smokey (Labina Mitevská) singing in a club of some sort, the whole bathed in a blue light. The plot proper is then set in motion with the cheerless return to Farhaven of a man who will be shortly identified as Martin. The film, in the manner to which classic Hollywood cinema has habituated us, leads us to ask questions about him: who is he? Where has he come from? Why is he stopping off at this seaside town? We are invited to hypothesise but are not given much information with which to do so. This series of elliptic images, of roads, truck and train, of a bag being dropped on the road when the man gets down from the truck, draws us in with its minimalism. Are there affiliations with those *noir* heroes returning to complete unfinished business or looking for direction in a world from which they feel alienated? Some of our questions are answered in the sequence shortly after in which Martin is seen with his probation officer (Geraldine O'Rawe), who is both attracted to him and determined to warn him about keeping out of trouble. But what sort of trouble?

And so the film, to this point, conforms to the expectations of melodrama, in narrative terms, but there is from the start a look to the film that gnaws away at one's confidence of having identified the mode. Winterbottom, immeasurably aided by Polish cinematographer Slawomir Idziak,[10] lingers over images of vast sky and sea, of small figures placed in formidable landscapes, of moving vehicles and the freeways they travel over. In this way, one is reminded of *Butterfly Kiss* (there are other echoes, too, of this film) in which the setting is at once realist and deformed by a highly personal vision. Here, though the representation of town and beach is clearly recognisable, it is also true, as one reviewer wrote, that 'he creates a world that's unfamiliar, post-apocalyptic but also grimly prosaic',[11] drawing attention accurately to the difficulty viewers may have, early in the film at least, in orienting themselves, not just to matters of ambience but also generically. Complicating further the film's reception as either a realist piece or a romantic melodrama is the way Idziak's camera bathes the screen in, say, yellow or a warm orange or chilly blue to signify shifts in mood. Mood, in fact, dominates one's impressions of the film, far more than response to either a tightly organised plot or a strict sense of verisimilitude. An Australian reviewer attributed much of the film's effect (and affect) to Idziak's idiosyncratic cinematography: 'Idziak creates pictures that don't simply tell the story – a downbeat tale about sad, dislocated lives – but demand to be framed and hung in an art gallery'.[12] The same writer goes on to note the ways 'in which the past and the future, like Idziak's mesmerising watery images, blur and bleed into each other'.[13]

Curiously, Winterbottom and screenwriter Eoin McNamee work to keep Martin and Helen apart for the first half of the film. A range of other relationships is established in the space between the two whom we take to be the protagonists. One of the most significant is that between Honda and his sister Smokey, who works as a singer at the pier club, and she and her frequent one-night stands have vigorous congress on the other side of the wall from where Honda sleeps – or records and/ or listens to what goes on in other people's relationships. In the *noir* paradigm, Smokey is what used to be called 'the lady of easy virtue', but she is also outgoing, frank and generous in her sexuality and genuinely fond of her mute brother, whom she cuddles to her bare breasts. She offers herself openly to Martin, who says he is attracted but who is too obsessed with the idea of Helen to respond. He has, meanwhile, engaged in mainly voyeuristic sexual activities with a stripper whom he has hired because she conforms to Helen's physical description. These scenes are strangely erotic and yet devoid of obvious sexual charge: the stripper's mind, even as she allows Martin to nuzzle her crotch, is clearly else- where. Elvis Costello's singing of the title song on the soundtrack works ironically in relation to this sequence but resonates with Martin's obses- sive passion for Helen, and it will be heard again over their last meeting. In fact, as Derek Elley reported, this '1986 song of obsessive love and erotic attraction was the jumping-off point for the whole project'.[14] And Winterbottom himself confirmed the song's importance: 'With a song you don't need to know all the background story; it's just the mood that draws you in'.[15]

Helen's secret is that it is she who has killed her father and let Martin take the blame and do the prison sentence. She finally tells this to Honda who has been collecting newspaper articles about the crime and Martin's role in it. When Martin finally comes to her, she taunts him with 'only want[ing] to fuck' her, as he had done nine years ago when she was fourteen; he wants her to say she loves him. He becomes violent; the furtively watching Honda comes to her rescue; and, when she batters Martin to death, she and Honda dispose of the body. In a near-repetition of the crime nine years earlier, Helen has not been convicted of the murder: Smokey's voice is heard comforting Honda with, 'The police went to Helen's house but they think it's self-defence', and Helen has disappeared. The *noir* scenario of the returning man and the ambiguous woman has arrived at a more than usually desolate ending. The reviewer who wrote that the film 'mainly holds one's interest because the story is so oddly told' is near the truth, as he was to continue with, 'all the characters seem to have dark sides ready to burst open at any time'.[16]

It is a film of subtly changing moods rather than a series of tight, causally connected events. It is this tonal bleakness and ambiguity which allies *I Want You* with *film noir*, as much as its more obvious resonances of character and incident. Certainly the stranger coming into the sleepy seaside town recalls the likes of Robert Ryan (on a different mission of course) in Fred Zinnemann's *Act of Violence* (1948) coming to disturb small-town domesticity, or just recently Ed Harris performing a similar function in David Cronenberg's *A History of Violence* (2005), and any number of revenants in between. In the history of British *noir*, precedents for this plot-opener are found in such films as Robert Hamer's *It Always Rains on Sunday* (1947), and, overlaid with post-war malaise, in Lance Comfort's *Silent Dust* (1948) and Cavalcanti's *They Made Me a Fugitive* (1948), or Terence Fisher's symptomatically titled *The Stranger Came Home* (1954). In terms of beautiful women who use their sexuality to ambivalent ends, Rachel Weisz's Helen is a linear descendant of such duplicitous *noir* ladies as Ava Gardner in Robert Siodmak's *The Killers* (1946) and Jane Greer in Jacques Tourneur's *Out of the Past* (1947), and the latter has a sombre ending akin to that of *I Want You*. But potent as these echoes are, and there are many more, it is the mood and moodiness of such British films as Mike Hodges' *Get Carter* (1971) and *Croupier* (1997), or Neil Jordan's *Mona Lisa* (1987), that *I Want You* most potently recalls. In a recent study, Andrew Spicer has summed up astutely the defining characteristics of British 'neo-noirs' in a way that is wholly apposite in relation to *I Want You*:

> the vast majority of British neo-noirs are variations of the crime thriller, differentiated from more conventional films by their highly wrought visual style, an emphasis on moral ambiguity and psychological complexity, and often deliberate blurring of the boundaries between reality and fantasy, subjectivity and objectivity.[17]

I Want You may be thought of as minor Winterbottom but it *is* unmistakably his. It is a film rich in intertextual references, not just those of the *noir* kind adverted to above; Jane Cornwell was right in identifying it as being 'influenced by American small-town thrillers and the European perspective of Smokey and Honda [to create] ... a mixed bag of a film'.[18] Like *Butterfly Kiss*, it is fascinated by the idea of strong women who will go to extreme lengths to assert their autonomy, and both end with such women committing acts of violence against men, and both end on utterly unromantic notes of desolation. In iconographic terms, both register a striking sense of modern anomie, of young people adrift in a society that renders their passions dangerous, a heedless society that is perhaps symbolised by the rawness of concrete freeways and, in *I Want You* particularly, by the recurring images of small human figures against large empty land- and seascapes. Again, as in so many of Winterbottom's films, there is an intensely kinetic effect of characters on the move, whether on freeways or bicycle paths or beaches or streets, but with no guarantee of any rewarding arrival. Martin's return, Honda and Helen's collision, Bob's pursuit of Honda over the shingles: these are metonymic representations of the dangerous possibilities of the restless movement that characterises so many of Winterbottom's films, from *Butterfly Kiss* and *Jude*, through *Welcome to Sarajevo* and *The Road to Guantánamo*. All these films offer a powerful sense of places and of the movement between them. In *I Want You*, the characters who are glimpsed as anchored to the one place tend to be elderly, like the old man (Graham Crowden) to whom Honda brings odd-shaped stones from the beach, or the gossiping women (Phyllida Law and Mary MacLeod) in the hairdressing salon. In Winterbottom's films, to be young is to be on the move: stasis belongs to those for whom the prospects of engagement are limited by age, rather than by contentment: merely being young, however, is no guarantee of buoyancy or even of survival.

Insofar as his films, in whatever genre-mix, offer any sort of coherent world view, it seems essentially a sombre one, and this is certainly true of *I Want You*. The reviewer who found it 'a dark, difficult and frankly depressing tale' but that 'it is also possessed of an eerie atmospheric quality which makes it curiously compelling'[19] came near to capturing its strange hold on the viewer. And as Derek Malcolm observed, 'It is about the most un-British film I've ever seen from a British director – and he would probably regard that as a compliment'.[20] If it is not wholly successful, it is more interesting than many stylistically and thematically less complex films which achieve simpler aims.

With or Without You

Winterbottom made his name on a series of television documentaries on Swedish filmmaker Ingmar Bergman. As Caroline Frost, writes: 'like the great Swede, Michael Winterbottom is striving time and time again to cast an ordinary landscape in a stunning new light'.[21] Putting to one side what this may imply in metaphoric terms, in the most literal way he does insist that we take serious notice of the landscape/townscape in which his generically eclectic films are set. His use of Hastings and Dungeness in *I Want You* is a significant element in the film's strange moody power, and that of Belfast in *With or Without You* is a good place to begin a discussion of this least-seen of Winterbottom's films. 'As in the films that came before it [*I Want You*], the environment the characters inhabit partakes significantly in the situations portrayed'.[22] The same is true of *With or Without You*, made primarily for television but given some theatrical screenings. The presence of Belfast is unemphatically insisted on (oxymoronic, one realises, but true).

It is in fact one of the strongest characteristics of Winterbottom's *oeuvre*: this insistence that all his films have on situating and representing their stories within the location and local history to which they belong. ('A sense of place is palpable in most of Winterbottom's films',[23] a recent essay claims.) In *With or Without You*, this is conveyed by Rosie (Dervla Kirwan) to her French former pen-pal Benoit (Yvan Attal) as the pair eat lunch at Belfast's Arc Brasserie in the Waterfront Hall development in Lanyon Place. Completed in 1997, just prior to the production of *With or Without You*, this development is part of the New Belfast; the Waterfront Hall can be seen as part of the worldwide phenomenon of redeveloping waterside and outmoded docklands. Previously shipyards, the Lanyon Place area alongside the Lagan River was seen at the time as a symbol of the transformation of Belfast from an industrial manufacturing centre to its membership of the new Europe community. In *With or Without You*, Rosie and Vincent (Christopher Eccleston) represent a young aspirant couple at the mercy of the same economic and cultural forces that saw the emergence of the European Economic Community. In this scene, Rosie introduces Belfast to Benoit from the vantage point of the Waterfront Hall development, pointing out the Lagan River, Harland and Wolff and Cave Hill, including Napoleon's Nose. She also points down to indicate the Waterfront Hall and remarks, 'And this used to be the bus station where I had my first kiss. Not very romantic', before returning to the tour, pointing to her left: 'Those over there are the Royal Courts of Justice and just behind those, the College of Knowledge [Belfast Metropolitan College] where I was going when I lived with Cathy'. To which Benoit responds: 'Is that when you met Vincent?' 'Yep, the first time was in Lavary's [a renowned Belfast bar], it's just behind there, you can't see it'. As this conversation takes place, the camera works its way in a slow 180 degree arc from left to right before resting on a close-up of Rosie's face.

At the completion of her micro-history, the conversation moves to Benoit's relationship with Caroline (Katia Caballero), while we witness nine 'objective' shots of the Lanyon Place district. This scene is a compendium of personal history closely tied to location and memory. Rosie's relating of her meeting of Vincent and the concomitant loss of her friendship with Cathy (Julie Graham) is, in this scene, inseparable from the old Belfast, her youth at the bus station now gone and Lavary's and the College of Knowledge, in this case, out of view. As part of this roll-call of memory names, Rosie includes Harland and Wolff, the Belfast ship-building dynasty, makers of the *Titanic*, whose shipyards on Belfast's Queen's Island are making way for a technology district designed to mirror the success of Dublin's IT-led renaissance. In all, this scene is melancholy, replete with an unstated romantic longing for a time prior to the pressures of marriage that seems inseparable from the tenor of the new Belfast, back to a time when Rosie and Benoit were simple pen-pals.

One can imagine a case mounted for the gratuitousness of some of the screen-time in which the camera quietly caresses the cityscape, but it is more important to consider *why* Winterbottom does so. There are traces of British New Wave practice here, as was noted in reference to *Go Now*, and which is also true of *I Want You*. Bristol, Hastings and Belfast are precisely encoded as participants in their respective films, but there is nevertheless something curiously muted about the uses to which these urban milieux are put. There is not even the implied leftist understanding of cramped lives as represented in those rows of bleak terraces and belching chimney-stacks one sees in the likes of *Room at the Top* (1958) and the films that followed. Rather, there is a quiet acceptance of the fact people are in part products of their characteristic environments, that they may be changed by these, that they may find themselves at odds with them or draw comfort from knowing them intimately. Belfast is a fact of life for Rosie and Vincent, both as a totality and in specific relation to the areas of their working lives, as it cannot be for Benoit, who remains an exotic there. This is not a political film, or at least not more so than one might describe any film's interaction of the individual and the community as political, but the tiny, just-audible radio reference to Gerry Adams and David Trimble (who'd shared a Nobel Peace Prize the year before) acts as a subtle signifier of the larger world. The reviewer who wrote the following was right: 'Its setting is one of the best things about the film. The Troubles are hardly mentioned; like the Bristol of *Go Now*, the city is just a place where people live, not a heavyweight symbol'.[24] Winterbottom's Belfast is palpable, not portentous.

If one starts an account of *With or Without You* by stressing Belfast, this may be because, like *I Want You*, it is stronger on ambience than narrative. In genre terms it is Winterbottom's only go at romantic comedy to date, but it is not really either very romantic or very comic. Its plot-launcher is announced in an early voice-over, during a concert; Rosie is heard saying: 'I was 29 years old. I'd known Vincent for ten years, we'd been married for five, but something was missing. We wanted a baby'. There's some lively cinematography and editing as the film flashes back to their sex life following the decision to try for pregnancy. 'Swim, you little bastards', Vincent orders his sperm in mid-sex. As one account of his films says: 'A number of Winterbottom's films deal with a very contemporary sense of male inadequacy and anxiety',[25] and nowhere is the issue more explicitly confronted than here. The doctor they consult suggests they consider a donor, an idea Vincent refuses to contemplate, and significantly this segment is immediately followed by the arrival of Benoit, who's come from France in search of Rosie. There are then brief segments of Rosie at work as receptionist at a gallery and Vincent, ex-cop, working with his glazier father-in-law Sammy (Alun Armstrong). We know by this time enough about the lives of Rosie and Vincent to be ready for the disruptive effect of Benoit's presence. In a moment that makes fun of sex, which *9 Songs* will later take so solemnly, Benoit, having located Rosie at the gallery, pokes his head into one of the exhibits: a large white furry simulacra of women's genitals. It's comic enough, but perhaps like so much of the early part of the film it is also more explicit than it needs to be.

In plot terms, there is a clear parallel intended in the functions of Benoit and Rosie's former friend, Cathy, a hairdresser, like Rachel Weisz's character in the preceding film and Shirley Henderson in his next, *Wonderland*. Vincent grows resentful of Benoit's presence in their flat, and eventually Rosie, furious at finding Vincent has been with Cathy, leaves with Benoit who has awakened repressed longings in her. They share an idyll in a forest out of the city and the setting is symptomatic of the 'naturalness' that has gone out of her and Vincent's increasingly programmed, even angry love-making. Cathy, Vincent's previous girl-friend who has resented Rosie's marrying him, seduces him effortlessly as he comes to repair a deliberately broken window in the room above the salon. The release that Rosie and Vincent find elsewhere (as distinct from the midday 'shag-break' they've been relentlessly pursuing) – and there is something too schematic about this plotting – leads finally to reaffirmation of their love. They get news that Rosie is after all this time pregnant, and the film ends with the christening and a group photo which suggests a moment frozen in time.

The working out of the narrative as it moves to its predictable closure is short on surprises, but romantic comedies have been made to work on premises no more intricate or substantial than John Forte's screenplay offers here. A more serious defect is that it is all apt to be more painful than funny. At one point when Vincent is going off to golf with his former police mates, Rosie jeers: 'It's not as if you really like golf. It's just an excuse to dress up in silly clothes. Why don't you join the Orange Order and be done with it?' Touches of wit like this, or like the disaffected Rosie striking back at her gallery boss over the paging system, 'Mr Ormonde, your prostitute has arrived', are rare enough to make one notice them and to reflect that snappy dialogue is not just an optional extra in romantic comedy. 'Actual jokes remain extremely thin on the ground',[26] a video reviewer remarked succinctly. Prodigiously and variously gifted as Winterbottom so clearly is, one can't help wondering if he has a touch light enough for this genre, if in fact he's not straining to make it into something bleaker, then pulling back with not always well-judged comic moments, as when Vincent pistol-whips Benoit when he finds him with Rosie in the forest. In a recent survey of the top twenty-one British directors, one critic had this to say of Winterbottom who came in twelfth:

> In contrast to many directors on this list, Winterbottom is dauntlessly prolific. Also, dauntingly versatile. He moves with consummate ease from literary adaptation (*Jude*, 1996) to pop-culture follies (*24 Hour Party People*, 2002) and excoriating social drama (*In This World*, 2002), and then back to the Eng Lit canon with his cunningly postmodern take on Tristram Shandy (*A Cock and Bull Story*, 2005).[27]

True enough, but the author of this comment wisely didn't include 'romantic comedy' in the 'versatile' list. Geoffrey Macnab reviewing the film on video release felt that 'Winterbottom ... never seems at home with the throwaway nature of the storyline'.[28] Perhaps in fairness, it might be added that neither of his leads, Eccleston, whom he used in *Jude* and who has a cameo in *24 Hour Party People*, nor Kirwan, both of them attractive enough performers, seems especially at home in the genre and they don't suggest between them the effortless chemistry it generally requires of its leads. Eccleston, a major figure in British cinema since the early 1990s, has a notably intense persona, which is probably better suited to the likes of *Jude* or the blacker comedy of Danny Boyle's *Shallow Grave* (1994). It is possible that these intertextual references work against one's easy acceptance of him as Vincent. Kirwan's main work has been on television, best remembered as pub-keeping Assumpta in *Ballykissangel* (1996–99) or the endangered heroine of *The*

Dark Room (1999). Individually, they are convincing enough in *With or Without You*; as a pair, they lack an essential rapport.

A positive review of the film in *Variety*, noting Winterbottom's way of suffusing his films with 'a distinctly European sensibility', drew attention to the film's freewheeling visual style: 'He uses split screen and even old-fashioned irises for emphasis and punctuation, and handles the material with freshness and vitality'.[29] Another reviewer, however, simply dismissed its visual habits as 'wilfully old-fashioned style tricks'.[30] One could argue that romantic comedy is one of the screen's oldest staples, and that the employment of some of its characteristic camera and editing devices draws attention to its intended generic lineage. Or that, as one critic has said: 'its frequent stylistic flourishes embody the director's ongoing resistance to presenting a narrative in a strictly conventional way'.[31] There may also be a nod to French New Wave practices, but, whatever *hommages* are intended, there is a sense of their decking out a slight scenario rather than belonging organically to its purposes. And the music, oddly for a Winterbottom film, seems almost casually added: Benoit gets misty-eyed during a Schubert string quintet; U2 does the title song on the soundtrack as Benoit and Rosie drive off together, but, from the director who so integrated the music and the drama in *24 Hour Party People*, it seems a little perfunctory. One critical assessment claims that Winterbottom 'has yet to make anything approaching a "feelgood" movie':[32] in most circumstances, one would take this as a compliment, but maybe for romantic comedy to work this needs to be factored in.

With or Without You is a minor entry in the director's canon. It has some delectable moments, like for instance those involving Vincent's golfing chums or Rosie with her work-mates (including the droll Doon MacKichan, from TV's *Smack the Pony*) or the lunch with Rosie's family, when everyone insists on talking about babies, or the scenes in Cathy's salon. In other words, the film is at its best in filling in the environment (urban and personal) of its protagonists, rather than in the emotional shading of their relationship with its desires and frustrations.

Conclusion

The films discussed in this chapter have some interests in common, without their constituting anything as coherent as a sub-genre. *9 Songs*, dealt with in detail in Chapter 2, is more of an oddity than the other three, even less readily classifiable. It is on one level a sex drama, but even to use the word 'drama' implies a kind of narrative organisation beyond what is on offer: that is, nine gigs separating scenes of actual sex. And yet, though there is no screenplay credit, there is a vestigial sense of narrative. The opening and near-closing shots of the male protagonist's life in the Antarctic, from which he looks back on the film's sex affair, are striking in themselves but hardly enough to provide more than a perfunctory context for the rest. The music is treated with an interest equal to that accorded the sex scenes – one hesitates to speak of it as a love affair – there's some tenderness but hardly enough emotional specificity to draw one into the relationship. As in so many of Winterbottom's films, and certainly in all four discussed in this chapter, there are insistent stress on movement, an almost mandatory beach scene (not just in these four films but also in *Jude*) as a somewhat simplistic signifier of release and 'naturalness', and stress on music. *9 Songs* isn't organised enough to share the melodramatic pull of, say, *I Want You*; the characters aren't sufficiently defined to promote the affective potency of *Go Now*; and it lacks even the intermittent comic invention in the central relationship that one occasionally finds in *With or Without You*, but as a quartet these films have just enough points of contact for us not to forget who made them.

Notes

1 Andrew Eaton, interview (May 2006).
2 Allison, 'Michael Winterbottom'.
3 Andrew Eaton, interview (May 2006).
4 Constantine Verevis, *Film Remakes*, p. 84. Verevis, in turn, draws on Rick Altman, 'A Semantic/Syntactic Approach to Film Genre', in Barry Keith Grant (ed.), *Film Genre Reader II* (Austin: University of Texas Press, 1995).
5 Ciment and Tobin, 'Entretien avec Michael Winterbottom', p. 26.
6 Now an historic shot as the skyline completely changed with the Harbourside Redevelopment of the 1990s. We are indebted to Andrew Spicer for identifying aspects of Bristol used in the film.
7 Franck Garbarz, '*Go Now*: La Maladie dangereuse', *Positif*, 430 (December 1996), pp. 19, 20.
8 *Variety* (28 August 1995), p. 65.
9 Derek Elley, *Variety* (23 February 1998), p. 80.
10 Idziak received a 'Special Mention' at the Berlin International Film Festival, 1998, for his work on *I Want You*.
11 Charlotte O'Sullivan, *Sight and Sound* (November 1998), p. 55.
12 Mark Naglazas, 'Through a Lens Darkly', *West Australian* (14 December 1998), p. 6.
13 *Ibid.*
14 Elley, *Variety*, p. 80.
15 Quoted in Jane Cornwell, 'The Winterbottom Line', *Sunday Age* (Melbourne) (4 October 1998), 'Applause', p. 7.
16 Dennis Schwartz, www.sover.net/~ozus (23 August 2001, accessed 8 April 2007).

17 Andrew Spicer, 'British Neo-noir', in Andrew Spicer (ed.), *European Film Noir* (Manchester: Manchester University Press, 2007), p. 112.

18 Cornwell, 'The Winterbottom Line', p. 7.

19 Caroline Westbrook, *Empire* (November 1998), p. 46.

20 Derek Malcolm, *The Guardian* (21 February 1998), p. 7.

21 Caroline Frost, Report of *Michael Winterbottom Profile*, BBC Two (16 January 2004).

22 Allison, 'Michael Winterbottom'.

23 Sinyard and Williams, '"Living In a World That Did Not Want Them": Michael Winterbottom and the Unpopular British Cinema', p. 119.

24 Lee Marshall, *Screen International*, 1229 (8–14 October 1999), p. 50.

25 Sinyard and Williams, '"Living In a World That Did Not Want Them": Michael Winterbottom and the Unpopular British Cinema', p. 118.

26 C. C., 'Comedy', *Empire* (April 2000), p. 110.

27 S. J., *The Telegraph* (14 April 2007), www.telegraph.co.uk/arts/ (accessed 23 April 2007).

28 Geoffrey Macnab, 'Rental Premiere', *Sight and Sound* (April 2001), p. 65.

29 David Stratton, *Variety* (6–12 September 1999), p. 64.

30 Marshall, *Screen International*, p. 50.

31 Allison, 'Michael Winterbottom'.

32 Sinyard and Williams, '"Living In a World That Did Not Want Them": Michael Winterbottom and the Unpopular British Cinema', p. 115.

Conclusion:
doing what you want to do

Despite modest financial return, Winterbottom's films have been well received, critically. Virtually none of his films has been given a critical thumbs-down; equally, though, none has been a major box-office hit. When this situation was put to producer Andrew Eaton, he had this to say:

> We do pretty good international sales so the films usually at least break even. The only one we've done that people had a problem with was *The Claim* which was just that higher level of budget and MGM released it in America with a view to try and garner some nominations and once you don't get those you're just left high and dry. So that film was probably one that lost money but we've managed to do them for reasonable enough budgets for it to not be too high a risk. That's especially true of *In This World* and *The Road to Guantánamo*, which were made from such low budgets that people made money from them.[1]

As the preceding chapters have indicated, the reviews, since the days of *Butterfly Kiss* and *Jude*, have tended to praise Winterbottom and the Revolution enterprise. No one at this stage is likely to expect of Winterbottom that he will be found directing a crowd-pleasing, special effects-driven spectacular, though, as also noted earlier, no one should ever be surprised at where he will strike next. His idiosyncratic way of taking on and refurbishing popular genres and making something new of them leads one to suppose that, if he took on making, as it were, *Spiderman 4*, it would look more than a little unlike its predecessors in the franchise.

His current standing in British film production is high. His latest release at time of writing, *A Mighty Heart*, not available for the present study, has won golden opinions at the Cannes Film Festival and there has been talk of Oscar nomination for its star, Angelina Jolie. The film, shot with characteristic Winterbottom eclecticism, in Texas, and several locations in India, Pakistan and France, has – and this is also characteristic – not produced a box-office success to match its critical reception. *Variety*, reporting its 'weak opening' in the US (it is a UK/US co-production), also reported: '"Mighty Heart" took in $5.4 million for its June 22 opening weekend, drawing a disappointing per-screen average of $2,914. In its second frame, the tally was $1.6 million'.[2] With a budget estimated at $16,000,000,[3] it is clear that it may take some time for the film to go into profit. However, this budgetary figure, and one allows for a certain looseness, still indicates that Winterbottom and Revolution Films are a very long way from those hugely lavish Hollywood spectacles that cost between one- and two-hundred million dollars and whose chief consideration is (the ephemera of) special effects. Paramount Vantage, the US company involved in this co-production with Revolution, with an eye to marketing the film in the States and perhaps acknowledging its special qualities, decided to engage in what is 'basically a retroactive platform release' which involved, after the first disappointing weekend's returns, to 'cut [...] back the number of screens from 1,350 to 651' to 'keep the film … alive in urban and other key markets with the goal of a longer box-office run'.[4]

The point of quoting this marketing information about the film is to highlight the recurring difficulties which must be faced by so prolific and uncompromising a director as Winterbottom. Revolution does seem to be an economically run production unit, those in charge appear more concerned with making films than fortunes, but, on the other hand, filmmaking and the arranging of distribution and exhibition are inevitably expensive operations. One is therefore impressed with Revolution's capacity to keep producing films of such quality without lowering of artistic standards, or, it seems, of personal and professional integrity. Scarcely one of its films can have seemed like obvious box-office material. Even when Winterbottom has embarked on that standby of British cinema, the adaptation of classic literature, his choices have been far from obvious: he has taken on two of Hardy's – and the nineteenth century's – bleakest protagonists in making *Jude* and *The Claim*, and no one filming *Tristram Shandy* could be said to opt for the easily accessible. When he has made road movies, they have been spiked with terminal pain in each of *Butterfly Kiss*, *In This World* and *The Road to Guantánamo*, and in the latter two at least, crossed with a documentary aesthetic that would seem to preclude the easy outcome of an upbeat ending. And the latter certainly also eludes his *noir* thriller, *I Want You*, and indeed most of his films.

These are films, that is, without the usual narrative safety nets. Further, their subject matter is often confronting in emotional impact and social implications. The (overtly) politically charged films – *Welcome*

to *Sarajevo*, *In This World* and *The Road to Guantánamo* – do not hesitate
to impugn repressive regimes or western complacency/opportunism
in the face of these. Only the comedies, *With or Without You* and *A
Cock and Bull Story*, could be said to give the audience an easier ride
from these points of view. However, the former is perhaps Winterbottom's least successful film, lacking real lightness of touch, and the
latter adopts such an intricately ludic approach, to what is already an
almost maniacally ludic text, that audiences expecting either comedy
or literary adaptation may well find themselves more than a little taxed
by its informing spirit of *jeu d'esprit*. In terms of characterisation, too,
he doesn't make life easy for viewers, generally eschewing the usual
empathy with protagonists that so much popular cinema has been built
on. One is hardly expected to warm to the Tim Robbins character who,
at the end of *Code 46*, is seen to be happily resettled with wife and child
while his lover, played by Samantha Morton, is exiled in a solitary desert
wasteland. Nor with the complexly interconnected and difficult lives of
the dwellers in the urban *Wonderland*; nor with the hairdresser protagonist in *I Want You* who, guilty of major crime, simply disappears at the
end. And the excoriating fates of Jude and Dillon, in the Hardy adaptations, leave one spent rather than exhilarated. At least a couple of the
other Revolution films on which Winterbottom has acted as Executive
Director, *Resurrection Man*, with its plot involving a violent murderer
in a Belfast Loyalist gang, and *Snow Cake*, with its alienated father and
autistic mother as protagonists, also gesture towards Winterbottom/
Revolution's avoidance of comforting scenarios.

From what one reads of *A Mighty Heart*, it seems to be very much
in line with many of its predecessors in the sense of not catering to
easy gratifications for audiences out for a good time. Like some of those
predecessors, it also sounds as if the filmmaker has been moved by a
real-life story. In Roger Ebert's words:

> The film is about the desperate search for Pearl (Dan Futterman) [a *Wall
> Street Journal* reporter and Winterbottom's third journalist protagonist]
> before the release of the appalling video showing him being beheaded. It
> is told largely through the eyes of and based on a memoir by his widow,
> Mariane.[5]

This is not, it seems, merely an exciting thriller set in exotic locations.
Ebert goes on to say that: 'Mariane Pearl's book, and the movie reminds
us, too, that some 230 other journalists had lost their lives at the time of
Pearl's kidnapping, most of them during the conflict in Iraq'. It sounds,
then, as if the film has some of the tonal complexity of those other politically charged films referred to above. Again, as another reviewer has
noted, the film recalls another of Winterbottom's skills:

For though his directing career has taken some strange turns ("Code 46," "9 Songs"), Winterbottom's strength, witness "The Road to Guantanamo" and especially "In This World," is his ability to create a phenomenal sense of place, especially where southern Asia is concerned.[6]

If it may be said that Winterbottom, with the backing of Revolution, has never sought to make the commercially more reliable projects that one might have expected as fill-ins between more intellectually and/ or emotionally taxing enterprises, it may also be argued that he and producer Eaton know what they are up to in industry terms. Look, for instance, at the budget figures quoted by the IMDb website for some of the films: at the upper end of the scale, *The Claim* was budgeted at an estimated $20m,[7] *Welcome to Sarajevo* cost $9m, and *Code 46*, with far-flung location work (China, India, United Arab Emirates, London, Hong Kong), was brought in for $7,500,000, while the opulent-looking *A Cock and Bull Story* cost only $2,800,000. At the other end of the scale, *In This World, 9 Songs* and *The Road to Guantánamo* were made for, respectively, $1,900,000, $1m, and $1,500,000. The purpose of quoting these figures (all of them described as 'estimated'[8]) is to suggest that, with such relatively modest budgeting, Winterbottom and Revolution can afford to ride out modest financial returns. According to Eaton, only in relation to their most expensive film to date, *The Claim*, has the budget/box-office disparity been really sobering. Angelina Jolie's name may be the draw for *A Mighty Heart*, but the mass audiences who might be expected to respond to her star power seem to have sniffed something more unsettling than her name may have initially suggested.

Winterbottom's next projects at the time of this writing are *Genova*, a ghost story in which a British man (Colin Firth) moves his daughters to Genoa following the death of his wife, and *Murder in Samarkand*. If the former suggests the possibility of uneasy emotional frissons, the latter, with a screenplay by David Hare (in itself enough to prepare one for discomfort), sounds very much like the line of territory that Winterbottom has mapped out on several occasions. It is based on the memoirs of the former British ambassador to Uzbekistan, Craig Murray, dismissed from his post for his outspoken criticism of Western backing of the country's violent rule. He is again venturing into dangerous territory – in terms both of content and of commercial returns – but that has never seemed to trouble him to date. The distinguished film writer David Thomson back in 2001 praised Winterbottom as one who 'deserves to be regarded as a very accomplished director who works in many moods', while acknowledging that 'There isn't an outright hit in that group [i.e., the films up to that time]'.[9] Perhaps, though, we might allow the last word to the director himself: in accounting in 2002 for taking on *In This World*, he told a reporter:

> Is it going to play in multiplexes? No, obviously not. Is it going to play anywhere? Probably not. But the point is it will be interesting to do, and, if you've got something interesting to do, then why wouldn't you want to do it? I want to do what I want to do rather than what's good for my career.[10]

Notes

1 Andrew Eaton, interview (May 2006).
2 Pamela McClintock, 'Paramount Tries "Heart" Surgery', *Variety* (21 May 2007), www.variety.com/review/VE1117933711.
3 See www.imdb.com/title/tt0829459/business (accessed 30 June 2007).
4 McClintock, 'Paramount Tries "Heart" Surgery'.
5 Roger Ebert, '*A Mighty Heart*' (22 June 2007), www.rogerebert.suntimes.com (accessed 30 June 2007).
6 Kenneth Turan, *Los Angeles Times* (22 June 2007), www.calendarlive.com (accessed 30 June 2007).
7 Winterbottom confirmed the figure as $21.3m in Simon Hatteston, 'Making It For Love Not For Money', *The Guardian*, reprinted in *The Sunday Age* (21 April 2002), p. 12.
8 See 'box-office/business' for individual titles at www.imdb.com or summarised under 'Budget' or 'Box-office' at www.pro.imdb.com/name (accessed 30 June 2007).
9 David Thomson, 'Thomas Hardy in a Cloak of Snow', *New York Times* (7 January 2001), AR 16.
10 Quoted in Hatteston, 'Making It For Love Not For Money', p. 12.

Epilogue

Winterbottom's UK/US co-production *A Mighty Heart* was not available for discussion in the texture of this book, but its appearance at the Melbourne International Film Festival in late July 2007 allows us to make brief reference to it in this Epilogue. Our chief aim is to suggest some of the ways in which its lineaments mark it unmistakably as a Winterbottom film.

First, it strikes one at once as yet another foray into politically dangerous territory. In this respect, it reminds one of *Welcome to Sarajevo*, which found drama in the war-torn Balkan states of the former Yugoslavia. And it looks forward to *Murder in Samarkand* (for 2008 release), in which western participation in the affairs of Third World countries will come under scrutiny. Between these two films, 'ripped from the headlines' as publicists are apt to say, came *In This World* and *The Road to Guantánamo*. In matters of theme and ideological preoccupation, it is possible to view it as the third in his series of films set in Asian countries (all are at least partly set and shot in Pakistan), where the threat of terrorism and the dubiety of western intervention create a perilous volatility. As one watches the alarming narrative of *A Mighty Heart* unfold, it is inevitable that those preceding films will colour one's reception of it.

There is a further echo of *Welcome to Sarajevo* in that its protagonist is again a journalist attempting to monitor this volatility, the while preserving a core of integrity, though *A Mighty Heart* has less of the conventional excitement of the man-in-a-fraught-situation than the earlier film. What they really share is a sense of the journalist's role in relation to the reporting of recent history, and, as in the other two Asian-set films referred to above, there is a pervasive aura of threat to the individual caught up in alarming events, caught as it were in the crossfire. Danny Pearl's situation in Pakistan is made the more dangerous by virtue of his Jewishness, which, as his wife says, he does not parade but equally would not deny. It is certainly no help to his project of investigating the link between shoe-bomber Richard Reid and militant Islamic groups. On his way to interview one Sheikh Gilani, he is last seen waiting outside the agreed restaurant, having been warned to stay in public places. This shot is inserted at later moments in the film as a poignant reminder of how unsafe the world can be for a decent man with a tricky mission. His western credentials – he is a writer for the *Wall Street Journal* – are no more help to him than the British nationality of the Tipton Three in *Guantánamo*.

Like those earlier films, *A Mighty Heart* shows Winterbottom in characteristically committed mode. Other directors may make sleeker films, films with fewer rough edges, but one regularly senses again in this new film the potent concern with issues of contemporary significance. Whereas it was a matter of the appalling privations endured by the refugees of *In This World* and the difficulty of finding justice in the face of intransigent western paranoia in *The Road to Guantánamo*, here he examines the parameters within which journalism must work if it is to report on matters of terrifying fact. Danny Pearl dies because he believes in his work and its importance in a world of half-understood threats and fears. The other protagonist, his wife Mariane, is also a journalist and, at the end of the film, a voice-over announces, 'She's still a journalist', as if to reinforce a belief in the value of the profession.

Behind the personal drama – the kidnapping of Danny, the frantic efforts to locate him, Mariane's pregnancy – hovers in the most minatory fashion the omnipresence of modern urban life. Contrasted with the vistas of historic Karachi, the mosques and minarets rising above the vast cityscape huddled below, is the sense of a world utterly – even frantically – dependent, at one level at least, on computers and cell phones, those desperate attempts at communication in a teeming world. In Winterbottom's 'Asian trilogy',[1] one is constantly made aware of the sheer difficulty of survival in overcrowded cities, and ways in which the west, so far from ameliorating such situations, has exacerbated them and insisted on maintaining its own higher living standards in stark contrast to the poverty and fear of those who have no choice but to live there or to try to escape.

Winterbottom is clearly fascinated by cities, not with any view to establishing their tourist marketability but to explore the ways in which they can constrict the lives of those who live there without the means to avail themselves of the best the cities can offer. The city doesn't have to be war-torn like Sarajevo, or a bureaucratic nightmare like Shanghai in *Code 46*, or the scary cocktail of appalling poverty, the whiff of terrorism and the westerners trying to deal with an elusive enemy in *A Mighty*

Heart; the featureless London streets of *Wonderland* or the end of *In This World* were already offering ample evidence for Winterbottom's view of metropolitan life. This view is at once fascinated and appalled.

This use of a threatening mise-en-scène, at its most alarming in *A Mighty Heart*, is characteristic of almost all of Winterbottom's work. As far back as his first feature, *Butterfly Kiss*, with its affectless stretches of motorways and the characterless strips of life along their edges, through the handsome quadrangles of learning that so firmly keep the protagonist at a distance in *Jude*, to the vast snowy emptinesses of *The Claim*, as well as the other films named above, he has always, more insistently than most directors, induced us to view his protagonists at the mercy of the worlds in which they find themselves. We discussed in chapter 2 two persistently recurring 'sites' in his work: the street and the body. His latest film could only have strengthened our case about his use of the street as a means of stressing that 'physical confrontation with the outside world'[2] which we noted earlier. It seems scarcely possible that movement can be sustained in the streets of Karachi: in one tense moment, Danny, on his way to meet the elusive Sheikh, sits tensely as his taxi is reduced to a standstill while buses, animals, carts, bicycles and cars jostle each other for a place in the road. And Karachi is represented with the same sense of documentary observation that characterised those earlier Asian-set films: it seems, though one knows that this is not so, as if we are being offered unmediated views of the city, without directorial intervention. This reminds one, too, of how he chose never to have London streets closed off for filming *Wonderland*, aiming instead for the authentic feel of crowded urban places, with their potential for the confusingly kinetic and their heedlessness of the personal and individual. Harlan Jacobson, reviewing the film, praised its director in these terms: 'Winterbottom, wielding his handheld hi-def camera on actual locations ..., is nothing if not superb at the ticktock of waiting for mayhem, at creating a milieu that feels like it's been ripped from the headlines [there's that phrase again] of CNN ...'.[3]

As for the emphasis on the 'body' as a site of drama in the film, Angelina Jolie's semi-transformation to suggest Mariane Pearl's Afro-Cuban heritage means that attention is focused on the slightly darkened skin, the prominent lips and the cascading black ringlets, as well as the swollen belly of her seven-month pregnancy. Nevertheless, as one online reviewer said of this 'physically and emotionally convincing' performance: 'A few obvious makeup changes make her resemble the woman we saw so often on TV ..., but Jolie's performance depends above all on inner conviction'.[4] In the mounting chaos and alarm surrounding the police search for Danny, she, in the sheer eloquence of her bodily presence, provides a powerful agent for coherence.

There are other reminders of whose film this is, apart from the menacing use of mise-en-scène. Among the personnel, we find Winterbottom regulars such as cinematographer Marcel Zyskind, editor Peter Christelis and casting director Wendy Brazington, as well as costume designer Charlotte Walter and actor Archie Panjabi, each on their second film for the director. In stylistic terms, the muted palette that has characterised films as diverse as *The Claim* and *In This World*, the use of voice-over that recalls Tony Wilson/Steve Coogan's soundtrack attempt to 'place' the events that make up *24 Hour Party People*, and the final long shot that reveals Mariane and her son walking in a Paris street, and lifts to lose them in the crowd, reminds one of the last moments of *Jude* and *The Claim*: in these and other ways, the Winterbottom signature is all over *A Mighty Heart*.

In other ways, it is also a step forward, a change of direction. While it is adapted from a literary work, this time the precursor is not a classic novel but Mariane Pearl's heartfelt memoir of her husband's life and hideous death. Whereas with the adaptation of a novel the filmmaker can feel as free as he likes in which elements of the antecedent text he chooses to emphasise, in relation to the filming of a real-life story, and a tragic one at that, one is reminded of David Lodge's comment on the writers of biography (as distinct from those of fiction): 'their liberty to shape their narratives ... is limited by a duty to historical truth-telling and the availability of evidence'.[5] What Winterbottom offers in *A Mighty Heart* is, then, a species of literary adaptation, yoked to techniques of documentary drama with an overriding social awareness – and perhaps for the first time, in the sheer physicality and emotional rigour of Jolie's performance, a star vehicle.

This latter element doesn't mean that he has produced a recognisable example of classical Hollywood narrative: the film depends too much on chaos and confusion for that. The whole, though, is a most potently organised amalgam of all those influences, and the very nature of the mix suggests that this least predictable of directors has surprised us yet again.

Notes

1 *Code 46* is of course partly set in Asia too, but for obvious genre reasons has less in common with the three designated here as Winterbottom's 'Asian trilogy'.
2 Douchet, *French New Wave*, p. 127.
3 Harlan Jacobson, 'A Mighty Heart', *Film Comment* (July–August 2007), p. 71.
4 Roger Ebert, 'A Mighty Heart' (22 June 2007), www.rogerebert.suntimes.com.
5 David Lodge, *The Year of Henry James* (London: Penguin Books, 2007), p. 30.

Filmography

Principal cast: Michael Elphick (Ken Boon), Neil Morrissey (Rocky), Harry Crawford (David Draker), Elizabeth Carling (Laura Marsh), Suzanna Hamilton (Judy), Stratford Johns (John), Samantha Morton (Mandy), Roger Lloyd-Pack (Ray Watts)

Dramarama: Rosie the Great, 1989

Production company: Thames Television
Producer: Richard J. Staniforth
Director: Michael Winterbottom
Director of photography: Ray Orton
Principal cast: Peter Capaldi

Inspector Alleyn Mysteries: Death at the Bar, 1990

Production company: BBC
Producer: George Gallaccio
Director: Michael Winterbottom
Screenplay: Alfred Shaughnessy
Director of photography: John Hawkins
Editor: Jackie Powell, Robin Graham Scott
Production designer: Martin Methven
Costume designer: Ken Trew
Music: Ray Russell
Sound: Steve Fish, Douglas Mawson
Principal cast: Patrick Malahide (Inspector Alleyn), William Simons (Inspector Fox), Kate Hardie (Decima Pomeroy), David Calder (Robert Legge), Alex Jennings (Sebastian Parish), Ben Daniels (Norman Cubitt), Anna Cropper (Violet Duffy)

Forget About Me, 1990, 72 min. (UK/Hungary)

Production company: Thames Television, Magyar Televízió Mûvelõdési Fõszerkesztõség (MTV)
Producer: Richard Handford
Director: Michael Winterbottom
Screenplay: Frank Cottrell Boyce
Director of photography: Ray Orton
Editor: Olivia Hetreed
Production designer: Katalin Kalmár
Costume designer: Philip Crichton, Eva Zalavari
Principal cast: Ewen Bremner (Broke), Brian McCardie (Bunny), Zsuz-

sanna Várkonyi (Czilla), Attila Grandpierre (Attila), Katalin Pataki (Anna)

Time Riders, 1991, 4 x 25 min.

Production company: Thames Television
Producer: Alan Horrox
Director: Michael Winterbottom
Screenplay: Jim Eldridge
Editor: Geraldine Phillips
Music: Debbie Wiseman
Production designer: Hayden Pearce
Principal cast: Haydn Gwynne (B. B. Miller), Clive Merrison (Professor Crow), Paul Bown (Captain), Ian McNeice (Leather Hardbones), James Saxon (Lord Chalmerston), Julie T. Wallace (Lady Chalmerston), Kenneth Hall (Ben Hardy), Kerry Swale (Hepworth), Gavin Richards (Witchfinder General)

Shrinks, 1991

Production company: Euston Films
Producer: Jackie Stoller
Director: Michael Winterbottom
Screenplay: Richard O'Keeffe, Jonathan Rich
Principal cast: Bill Patterson (Matt Hennessey), Yvonne Bryceland (Magda Myers), Patricia Kerrigan (Win Bargate), Brian Protheroe (Leo Brompton), Simon Jones (Jack Cavendish)

Under the Sun, 1991

Production company: Thames Television
Producer: Paul Horrocks
Director: Michael Winterbottom
Costume designer: Rachael Fleming
Sound: Aad Wirtz
Principal cast: Kate Hardie (Ellie), Stella Maris (Maria), Arturo Venegas (Felipe), Caroline Catz (Linda), Iker Ibáñez

Love Lies Bleeding, 1993, 89 min.

Production company: BBC
Producer: Robert Cooper

Director: Michael Winterbottom
Screenplay: Ronan Bennett
Director of cinematography: Eric Gillespie
Editor: David Spiers
Production designer: Tom McCullagh
Sound: Aad Wirtz
Principal cast: Mark Rylance (Conn), Elizabeth Bourgine (Sophie Allen), John Kavanagh (Sean Kerrigan), Brendan Gleeson (Thomas Macken), Tony Doyle (Geordie Wilson), Robert Patterson (Artie Flynn), George Shane (Gerry Ellis), James Nesbitt (Niall), Tim Loane (Robinson), Bosco Hogan (Rory McGinn), Margaret D'Arcy (Lily), Emma Jordan (Layla)

Cracker: 'The Mad Woman in the Attic', 1993, 100 min.

Production company: ITV
Producer: Gub Neal
Director: Michael Winterbottom
Screenplay: Jimmy McGovern
Director of photography: Ivan Strasburg
Editor: Trevor Waite
Costume designer: Tudor George
Art director: David Butterworth
Music: Julian Wastall
Principal cast: Robbie Coltrane (Dr Eddie 'Fitz' Fitzgerald), Barbara Flynn (Judith Fitzgerald), Christopher Eccleston (DCI David Bilborough), Lorcan Cranitch (DS Jimmy Beck), Geraldine Somerville (DS Jane Penhaligon), Kieran O'Brien (Mark Fitzgerald), Adrian Dunbar (Thomas Kelly), Kika Markham (Ann Appleby), John Grillo (Simon Appleby)

Family, 1994, 4 x 50 min. (UK/Ireland)

Production company: BBC
Producer: Andrew Eaton
Director: Michael Winterbottom
Screenplay: Roddy Doyle
Director of photography: Daf Hobson
Editor: Trevor Waite
Principal cast: Sean McGinley (Charlo Spencer), Ger Ryan (Paula Spencer), Barry Ward (John Paul Spencer), Neili Conroy (Nicola Spencer), Gemma Butterly (Leanne Spencer)

Cinema Europe: The Other Hollywood: 'Art's Promised Land', 1995, 60 min. (UK/France/Germany)

Production company: Photoplay Productions, Sept, Zweites Deutsches Fernsehen
Producers: David Gill, Kevin Brownlow
Director: Michael Winterbottom
Directors of photography: Jerker Nylen, Ulf Simonsson
Music: Philip Appleby
Consultant: Peter Cowie
Narrator: Kenneth Branagh
Participant: Claude Autant-Lara

Go Now, 1995, 81 min.

Production company: Revolution Films, BBC
Producer: Andrew Eaton
Director: Michael Winterbottom
Screenplay: Jimmy McGovern, Paul Henry Powell
Director of photography: Daf Hobson
Editor: Trevor Waite
Production designer: Hayden Pearce
Costume designer: Rachael Fleming
Music: Alastair Gavin
Sound: Martin Trevis
Principal cast: Robert Carlyle (Nick Cameron), Juliet Aubrey (Karen), James Nesbitt (Tony), Sophie Okonedo (Paula), Tom Watson (Bill Cameron), Barbara Rafferty (Madge Cameron), Berwick Kaler (Sammy), Darren Tighe (Dell), Sean McKenzie (George), John Brobbey (Geoff), Sara Stockbridge (Bridget), Tony Curran (Chris Cameron), Erin McMahon (Julie Cameron), David Schneider (doctor), Susie Fugle (scan doctor)

7 Days, begun in 2007

Production company: Channel 4
Director: Michael Winterbottom
Principal cast: John Simm, Shirley Henderson

Films

Butterfly Kiss, 1995, 85 min.

Production company: Dan Films, British Screen, Merseyside Film Production Fund
Producer: Julie Baines
Director: Michael Winterbottom
Screenplay: Frank Cottrell Boyce
Director of photography: Seamus McGarvey
Costume designer: Rachael Fleming
Editor: Trevor Waite
Production designer: Rupert Miles
Music: John Harle
Sound: Ronald Bailey
Principal cast: Amanda Plummer (Eunice), Saskia Reeves (Miriam), Kathy Jamieson (Wendy), Des McAleer (Eric McDermott), Freda Dowie (Elsie), Ricky Tomlinson (Robert), Paul Bown (Gary), Emily Aston (Katie), Lisa Jane Riley (Danielle), Paula Tilbrook (Ella), Joanne Cook (Angela), Katy Murphy (Judith)

Jude, 1996, 123 min.

Production company: Revolution Films, PolyGram Filmed Entertainment, BBC Films
Producer: Andrew Eaton
Director: Michael Winterbottom
Screenplay: Hossein Amini, from the novel by Thomas Hardy
Director of photography: Eduardo Serra
Editor: Trevor Waite
Production designer: Joseph Bennett
Costume designer: Janty Yates
Music: Adrian Johnston
Sound: Kant Pan, Jeremy Child
Principal cast: Christopher Eccleston (Jude Fawley), Kate Winslet (Sue Bridehead), Rachel Griffiths (Arabella), Liam Cunningham (Phillotson), June Whitfield (Aunt Drusilla), James Daley (Jude, as a boy), Ross Colvin Turnbull (little Jude), James Nesbitt (Uncle Joe), Paul Bown (Uncle Jim), Amanda Ryan (gypsy saleswoman), Vernon Dobtcheff (curator), David Tennant (drunk undergraduate), Freda Dowie (elderly landlady), Dexter Fletcher (priest), Ken Jones (Mr Biles), Paul Copley (Mr Willis)

Welcome to Sarajevo, 1997, 101 min. (UK/US)

Production company: Channel Four, Miramax Films, Dragon Pictures
Producer: Graham Broadbent, Damian Jones
Director: Michael Winterbottom
Screenplay: Frank Cottrell Boyce, based on *Natasha's Story* by Michael
  Nicholson
Director of photography: Daf Hobson
Editor: Trevor Waite
Production designer: Mark Geraghty
Costume designer: Janty Yates
Music: Adrian Johnston
Sound: Martin Trevis
Principal cast: Stephen Dillane (Michael Henderson), Woody Harrelson
  (Flynn), Marisa Tomei (Nina), Emira Nusević (Emira), Kerry Fox (Jane
  Carson), Goran Višnjić (Risto), James Nesbitt (Gregg), Emily Lloyd
  (Annie McGee), Juliet Aubrey (Helen Henderson), Igor Dzambazov
  (Jacket), Gordana Gadzic (Mrs Savic), Dražen Šivak (Zelkjo), Vesna
  Orel (Munira Hodzic)

I Want You, 1998, 87 min.

Production company: Revolution Films, PolyGram Films (UK) Ltd
Producer: Andrew Eaton
Director: Michael Winterbottom
Screenplay: Eoin McNamee
Director of photography: Slawomir Idziak
Editor: Trevor Waite
Production designer: Mark Tildesley
Costume designer: Rachael Fleming
Music: Adrian Johnston, Rare
Sound: Martin Trevis
Principal cast: Rachel Weisz (Helen), Alessandro Nivola (Martin), Labina
  Mitevská (Smokey), Luka Petrusic (Honda), Graham Crowden (old
  man), Ben Daniels (DJ Bob), Geraldine O'Rawe (Sonja), Carmen Ejogo
  (Amber), Des McAleer (florist), Phyllida Law, Mary MacLeod (salon
  customers), Steven John Shepherd (Sam), David Hounslow (Frank)

Resurrection Man, 1998, 102 min.

Production company: Revolution Films, PolyGram Films (UK)
Producer: Andrew Eaton
Executive producer: Michael Winterbottom

Director: Marc Evans
Screenplay: Eoin McNamee (from his book)
Director of photography: Pierre Aim
Editor: John Wilson
Production designer: Mark Tildesley
Costume designer: Nic Ede
Music: David Holmes, Gary Burns, Keith Tenniswood
Sound: Martin Trevis
Principal cast: Stuart Townsend (Victor Kelly), Geraldine O'Rawe
  (Heather Graham), James Nesbitt (Ryan), John Hannah (Darkie
  Larche), Brenda Fricker (Dorcas Kelly)

With or Without You, 1999, 90 min.

Production company: Revolution Films, FilmFour, Miramax Films
Producer: Andrew Eaton
Director: Michael Winterbottom
Screenplay: John Forte, Andrew Eaton
Director of photography: Benoît Delhomme
Editor: Trevor Waite
Production designer: Mark Tildesley
Costume designer: Janty Yates
Music director: Adrian Johnston
Sound: Martin Trevis
Principal cast: Christopher Eccleston (Vincent), Dervla Kirwan
  (Rosie), Yvan Attal (Benoit), Julie Graham (Cathy), Alun Armstrong
  (Sammy), Lloyd Hutchinson (Neil), Michael Liebmann (Brian),
  Doon MacKichan (Deidre), Gordon Kennedy (Ormonde), Fionnula
  Flanagan (Irene), Dan Gordon (Terry), Donna Dent (Lillian), Peter
  Ballance (Andrew), Ali White (Rosie's doctor), Alan McKee (passport
  official), Mike Dowling (minister), Katia Caballero (Caroline)

Wonderland, 1999, 108 min.

Production company: Revolution Films, PolyGram Films (UK) Ltd,
  Kismet Film Company, BBC Films, Universal Pictures International,
  British Screen Finance
Producer: Andrew Eaton, Michele Camarda
Director: Michael Winterbottom
Screenplay: Laurence Coriat
Director of photography: Sean Bobbitt
Editor: Trevor Waite

Production designer: Mark Tildesley
Costume designer: Natalie Ward
Music (composer): Michael Nyman
Sound: Richard Flynn
Principal cast: Shirley Henderson (Debbie), Gina McKee (Nadia), Molly Parker (Molly), Ian Hart (Dan), John Simm (Eddie), Stuart Townsend (Tim), Kika Markham (Eileen), Jack Shepherd (Bill), Enzo Cilenti (Darren), Sarah-Jane Potts (Melanie), David Fahm (Franklyn), Ellen Thomas (Donna), Peter Marfleet (Jack), Nathan Constance (Alex)

The Claim, 2001, 121 min.

Production company: Revolution Films, Kingdom Films, Pathé Pictures, United Artists Films, Arts Council of England, Studio Canal+, BBC Films, Alliance Atlantis, Grosvenor Park, Alberta Foundation for the Arts, Canadian Film and Television Production Tax Credit Scheme
Producer: Andrew Eaton
Director: Michael Winterbottom
Screenplay: Frank Cottrell Boyce, inspired by the novel, *The Mayor of Casterbridge* by Thomas Hardy
Director of photography: Alwin Küchler
Editor: Trevor Waite, and Larry Becker (Canada)
Production designer: Mark Tildesley
Costume designer: Joanne Hansen
Music: Michael Nyman
Sound: Ian Wilson (sound supervisor), Peter Christelis, Conor Mackey
Principal cast: Peter Mullan (Daniel Dillon), Wes Bentley (Dalglish), Nastassja Kinski (Elena Dillon), Sarah Polley (Hope Dillon), Milla Jovovich (Lucia), Sean McGinley (Sweetley), Shirley Henderson (Annie), Karolina Muller (young Elena), Kate Hennig (Vauneen), Marie Brassard (French Sue), Duncan Fraser (Crocker), Julian Richings (Ballanger)

24 Hour Party People, 2002, 115 min.

Production company: Revolution Films, Film Consortium, United Artists
Producer: Andrew Eaton
Director: Michael Winterbottom
Screenplay: Frank Cottrell Boyce
Director of photography: Robby Müller
Editor: Trevor Waite

Production designer: Mark Tildesley
Costume designer: Natalie Ward, Stephen Noble
Music supervisor: Liz Gallacher
Sound: Stuart Wilson
Principal cast: Steve Coogan (Tony Wilson), Lennie James (Alan Erasmus), Shirley Henderson (Lindsay Wilson), Paddy Considine (Rob Gretton), Andy Serkis (Martin Hannett), Sean Harris (Ian Curtis), John Simm (Bernard Sumner), Ralf Little (Peter Hook), Danny Cunningham (Shaun Ryder), Chris Coghill (Bez), Paul Popplewell (Paul Ryder), Keith Allen (Roger Ames), Rob Rydon (Ryan Letts), Enzo Cilenti (Peter Saville), Ron Cook (Derek Ryder), Dave Gorman (John the postman), Peter Kay (Don Tonay), Kate Magowan (Yvette Wilson), Kieran O'Brien (Nathan McGough), Simon Pegg (journalist), Rowetta (Rowetta), Paul Ryder (Pel), John Thomson (Charles), Raymond Waring (Vini Reilly), Nick Clarke (Gaz), Margi Clarke (actor in corridor), Toby Salaman (Sir Keith Joseph), Helen Schlesinger (Hilary), Christopher Eccleston (tramp)

Heartlands, 2002, 90 min. (UK/US)

Production company: Revolution Films, DNA Films, Miramax Films, Vestry Films
Producer: Gina Carter
Executive producer: Michael Winterbottom (and others)
Director: Damien O'Donnell
Screenplay: Paul Fraser, from story by Fraser and others
Director of photography: Alwin Küchler
Editor: Frances Parker
Production designer: Tom Conroy
Costume designer: Natalie Ward
Music: John McCusker, Kate Rusby
Sound: Zane Hayward
Principal cast: Michael Sheen (Colin), Mark Addy (Ron), Jim Carter (Geoff), Celia Imrie (Sonja), Mark Strong (Ian), Ruth Jones (Mandy)

Bright Young Things, 2003, 106 min.

Production company: Bright Young Films Limited, Works Production, Revolution Films, Doubting Hall
Producers: Gina Carter, Miranda Davis
Executive producers: Michael Winterbottom, Andrew Eaton (and others)
Director: Stephen Fry

Screenplay: Stephen Fry, from Evelyn Waugh's novel, *Vile Bodies*
Director of photography: Henry Braham
Editor: Alex Mackie
Production designer: Michael Howells
Costume designer: Nic Ede
Music: Anne Dudley
Sound: Jim Greenhorn
Principal cast: Emily Mortimer (Nina), Stephen Campbell Moore (Adam), Dan Aykroyd (Lord Monomark), Jim Broadbent (drunken major), Stockard Channing (Mrs Melrose Ape), James McAvoy (Lord Simon Balcair), Fenella Woolgar (Agatha)

Code 46, 2003, 93 min.

Production company: Revolution Films, UK Film Council, BBC Films, MEDIA Programme of the European Union, United Artists, National Film Trustee Company, Shanghai Film Studio.
Producer: Andrew Eaton
Director: Michael Winterbottom
Screenplay: Frank Cottrell Boyce
Director of photography: Alwin Küchler, Marcel Zyskind
Editor: Peter Christelis
Production designer: Mark Tildesley
Costumes: Natalie Ward
Music: The Free Association, David Holmes, Steve Hilton
Sound: Stuart Wilson
Principal cast: Tim Robbins (William), Samantha Morton (Maria Gonzalez), Jeanne Balibar (Sylvie), Essie Davis (doctor), Om Puri (Bahkland), Nabil Elouahabi (vendor), David Fahm (Damian Alekan), Shelley King (William's boss), Archie Panjabi (check-in), Kerry Shale (clinic doctor), Natalie Mendoza (Sphinx receptionist), Benedict Wong (medic)

In This World, 2003, 88 min.

Production company: Revolution Films
Producer: Andrew Eaton, Anita Overland
Director: Michael Winterbottom
Screenplay: Tony Grisoni
Director of photography: Marcel Zyskind
Editor: Peter Christelis
Music/Music conductor: Dario Marianelli

Principal cast: Jamal Udin Torabi (Jamal), Enayatullah (Enayat). *Pakistan*: Imran Paracha (travel agent), Hiddayatullah (Enayat's brother), Jamau (Enayat's father), Ahsan Raza (money changer), Mirwais Torabi (Jamal's older brother), Amanullah Torabi (Jamal's younger brother). *Iran*: Hossain Baghaeian (Behrooz), Yaaghoob Nosraj Poor (Kurdish father), Ghodrat Poor (Kurdish mother). *Turkey*: Kerem Atabeyoglu (policeman), Erham Sekizcan (factory boss). *Europe*: Nabil Elouahabi (Yusif), Paul Popplewell (voice-over)

9 Songs, 2004, 69 min.

Production company: Revolution Films
Producer: Andrew Eaton
Director: Michael Winterbottom
Director of photography: Marcel Zyskind
Editors: Mat Whitecross, Michael Winterbottom
Music: Black Rebel Motorcycle Club, The Von Bondies, Michael Nyman, Salif Keita, Elbow, Franz Ferdinand, Primal Scream, Melissa Parmenter, The Dandy Warhols, Goldfrapp, Super Furry Animals
Sound: Stuart Wilson
Principal cast: Kieran O'Brien (Matt), Margo Stilley (Lisa), Michael Nyman, Franz Ferdinand (on-screen music performers)

Hot Spot, 2004, 62 min.

Production company: Revolution Films, Top Spot Films, BBC (TV version)
Producer: Melissa Parmenter
Executive producer: Michael Winterbottom (and others)
Director: Tracey Emin
Screenplay: Tracey Emin
Director of photography: Sebastian Sharples
Music: Melissa Parmenter
Sound: Rashad Omar
Principal cast: Elizabeth Crawford (Lizzie), Laura Curnick (Laura), Katie Foster Barnes (Katie), Helen Laker (Helen), Keiri Noddings (Keiri), Frances Williams (Frances)

Goal!, 2005, 118 min. (UK/US/Japan)

Production company: Goal Limited, Milkshake Films
Director: Danny Cannon (Michael Winterbottom original director)

A Cock and Bull Story, 2006, 94 min.

Production company: Revolution Films, Scion Films, Baby Cow Productions, BBC Films, EM Media
Producer: Andrew Eaton
Director: Michael Winterbottom
Screenplay: 'Martin Hardy' (i.e., Frank Cottrell Boyce and Michael Winterbottom), from the novel by Laurence Sterne, *Tristram Shandy*
Director of photography: Marcel Zyskind
Editor: Peter Christelis
Production designer: John Paul Kelly
Costume designer: Charlotte Walter
Music: Michael Nyman (and others)
Sound: Stuart Wilson
Principal cast: Steve Coogan (Steve Coogan/Walter Shandy/Tristram Shandy), Rob Brydon (Rob Brydon/Uncle Toby), Keeley Hawes (Elizabeth Shandy), Shirley Henderson (Susannah/Shirley Henderson), Dylan Moran (Dr Slop), David Walliams (parson), Jeremy Northam (Mark, the director), Benedict Wong (Ed), Naomie Harris (Jennie, the runner), Kelly Macdonald (Jenny, Steve's girlfriend), Elizabeth Berrington (Debbie), Mark Williams (Ingoldsby), Kieran O'Brien (Gary), Roger Allam (Adrian), James Fleet (Simon, the producer), Ian Hart (Joe, the screenwriter), Ronni Ancona (Anita), Greg Wise (Greg), Stephen Fry (Patrick/Parson Yorick), Gillian Anderson (Widow Wadman/Gillian Anderson), Raymond Waring (Corporal Trim), Paul Kynman (Obadiah), Mark Tandy (London doctor), Jack Shepherd (surgeon)

The Road to Guantánamo, 2006, 95 min.

Production company: Revolution Films, Screen West Midlands, FilmFour
Producer: Andrew Eaton, Melissa Parmenter
Director: Michael Winterbottom, Mat Whitecross
Director of photography: Marcel Zyskind
Editor: Michael Winterbottom, Mat Whitecross
Production designer: Mark Digby
Costumes: Esmaeil Maghsoudi
Music: Molly Nyman, Harry Escott
Sound: Stuart Wilson
Principal cast: Rizwan Ahmed (Shafiq), Farhad Harun (Ruhel), Arfan Usman (Asif), Waqar Siddiqui (Monir), Shahid Iqbal (Zahid), Jason Salkey, Jacob Gaffney, Mark Holden (US interrogators), Duane Henry,

William Meredith, Payman Bina (military guards), Adam James (SAS interrogator), Ian Hughes (MI5 interrogator), Brian Flaherty, Steven Beckingham, Jason Schams, James Buller (camp X-ray guards), Mark Sproston (embassy man), Sara Stewart (Washington woman), Demitri Goritsas (Bashir), Sasha Pick (CIA woman)

Snowcake, 2006, 112 min. (UK/Can)

Production company: Revolution Films, Rhombus Media
Producers: Gina Carter, Andrew Eaton, Jessica Daniel, Niv Fichman
Executive producer: Michael Winterbottom (and others)
Director: Marc Evans
Screenplay: Angela Peel
Director of photography: Steve Cozens
Editor: Mags Arnold
Production designer: Matthew Davies
Costume designer: Debra Hanson
Music: Broken Social Scene
Sound: Paul Cottrell
Principal cast: Alan Rickman (Alex Hughes), Sigourney Weaver (Linda Freeman), Carrie-Anne Moss (Maggie), David Fox (Dirk Freeman), Jayne Eastwood (Ellen Freeman), Emily Hampshire (Vivienne Freeman), Selina Cadell (Diane Wooton)

A Mighty Heart, 2007, 100 min. (UK/US)

Production company: Revolution Films
Producer: Andrew Eaton
Director: Michael Winterbottom
Screenplay: John Orloff, from Marianne Pearl and Sarah Crichton's story, *A Mighty Heart: The Brave Life and Death of My Husband Danny Pearl*
Director of photography: Marcel Zyskind
Editor: Peter Christelis
Production designer: Marl Digby
Costume designer: Charlotte Walter
Music: Harry Escott, Molly Nyman
Sound: Rashad Omar
Principal cast: Angelina Jolie (Mariane Pearl), Dan Futterman (Danny Pearl), Will Patton (Randall Bennett), Archie Panjabi (Asra Q. Nomani), Azfar Ali (Asra'a boyfriend), Denis O'Hare (John Bussey), Zachary Coffin (Matt McDowell), Harvasp Chiniwala (Adam Pearl),

Demetri Goritsas (John Skelton), Jillian Armenante (Maureen Platt), Sajid Hasan (Zubair), Gary Wilmes (Steve Levine)

Murder in Samarkand, 2008

Production company: Revolution Films
Producer: Andrew Eaton
Director: Michael Winterbottom
Screenplay: David Hare, from Craig Murray's memoir, *Murder in Samarkand*
Principal cast: Steve Coogan (Craig Murray), Nadira Alieva

Select bibliography

Allison, Deborah, 'Michael Winterbottom' (May 2005), www.sense-sofcinema.com (accessed 25 July 2005).

Atkinson, Michael, 'Cinema as Heart Attack', *Film Comment* (January/February 1998), pp. 44–7.

Barthes, Roland, *Image-Music-Text*, trans. Stephen Heath (Glasgow: Collins/Fontana, 1977).

Bergala, Alain, 'The Other Side of the Bouquet' in Raymond Bellour with Mary Lea Bandy (eds), *Jean-Luc Godard: Son + Image 1974–1991* (New York: The Museum of Modern Arts, 1992), pp. 56–73.

Bergman, Ingmar, *Magic Lantern: An Autobiography*, trans. Joan Tate (London: Hamish Hamilton; New York: Viking Penguin, 1988).

Berthomieu, Pierre, '*Jude*: Vivantes couleurs', *Positif*, 430 (December 1996), pp. 17–18.

Bourdieu, Pierre, *The Field of Cultural Production*, ed. and trans. Randal Johnson (Cambridge: Polity Press, 1993).

Britain, Ian, 'Pastoral Images' in Brian McFarlane (ed.), *The Encyclopedia of British Film* [2003] (London: Methuen/BFI, 2nd edn, 2005), pp. 510–11.

Brown, Geoff and Pamela Church Gibson, 'Michael Winterbottom' in Robert Murphy (ed.), *Directors in British and Irish Cinema* (London: BFI Publishing, 2006), pp. 628–9.

Caughie, John, 'Don't Mourn – Analyse: Reviewing the Trilogy' in Eddie Dick, Andrew Noble and Duncan Petrie (eds), *Bill Douglas: A Lanternist's Account* (London: BFI Publishing, 1993) pp. 197–204.

Ciment, Michel and Yann Tobin, 'Des personages auxquels on refuse l'accès à la société » Entretien avec Michael Winterbottom', *Positif*, 430 (December 1996), pp. 23–8.

Comolli, Jean-Louis, 'Historical Fiction: A Body Too Much', *Screen*, 19: 2 (Summer 1978), pp. 41–53.

Corner, John, *The Art of Record: A Critical Introduction to Documentary* (Manchester: Manchester University Press, 1996).

Davis, Bob, 'A World Apart', *American Cinematographer*, 85: 9 (September 2004), pp. 56–60.

Douchet, Jean, *French New Wave*, in collaboration with Cédric Anger, trans. Robert Bonnono (New York: D.A.P./Distributed Art Publishers, Inc. in association with Éditions Hazan/Cinématèque Française, 1998).

Dyer, Richard, 'Entertainment and Utopia' in Rick Altman (ed.), *Genre: The Musical* (London and New York: Routledge & Kegan Paul/BFI, 1981), pp. 175–89.

Epstein, Jan, 'Welcome to Sarajevo', *Cinema Papers* (March 1998), pp. 28–30, 45.

Fennell, Nicky, 'Winter Wonderland', *Film West* (February 2000), pp. 42–4.

Feuer, Jane, *The Hollywood Musical* (London and Basingstoke: Macmillan Press/BFI, 1982).

Garbarz, Franck, '*Go Now:* La Maladie dangereuse', *Positif*, 430 (December 1996), pp. 19–20.

Gerhardt, Paul, Derek Jones and Edward Buscombe (eds), *Working with Ingmar Bergman: Interviews by Michael Winterbottom* (London: British Film Institute, 1988).

Gilbey, Ryan, 'Kinky Bio', *Sight and Sound* (April 2002), pp. 20–2.

—— *It Don't Worry Me: Nashville, Jaws, Star Wars and Beyond* (London: Faber and Faber, 2003).

—— 'British Directors: Open Mike', *Sight & Sound* (October 2004), pp. 30–4.

Hardy, Phil, 'The Science Fiction Film in Perspective' in Hardy (ed.), *The Aurum Film Encyclopedia: Science Fiction* (London: Aurum Press, 1984), pp. ix–xv.

Hardy, Thomas, *The Life and Death of the Mayor of Casterbridge* [1886] (London: Macmillan, 1947).

—— *Jude the Obscure* [1895] (London: Macmillan, 1956)

Heath, Stephen, 'The Question Oshima' in *Questions of Cinema* (London: Macmillan, 1981), pp. 145–64.

Hennigon, Adrian, 'Michael Winterbottom Interviewed, *BBC Movies*, www.bbc.co.uk/films/2005/03/03/michael_winterbottom_9_songs_interview.shtml.

Houllebecq, Michel, *Platform* [2001] (London: Vintage Books, 2003).

Jones, Kent, 'I Walk the Line', *Film Comment* (January/February 2005), pp. 30–3.

Koos, Leonard R., 'Films Without Borders', *Post Script*, 25: 2 (Winter–Spring, 2006), pp. 3–18.

Lovell, Alan, 'Free Cinema' in Alan Lovell and Jim Hillier, *Studies in*

Documentary Film (London: Secker and Warburg/British Film Institute, 1972), pp. 135–6.

Marie, Michel, *The French New Wave: An Artistic School* (Malden MA and Oxford: Blackwell, 2003).

Martin, Adrian, 'Refractory Characters: Shards of Time and Space', *Metro* (Melbourne) 100 (Summer 1994/95), pp. 40–8.

—— 'Ticket to Ride: Claire Denis and the Cinema of the Body', *Screening the Past: An International Refereed Journal of Visual Media and History*, 20 (2006) uploaded 11/12/2006, www.latrobe.edu.au/screeningthepast/20/claire-denis.html.

McFarlane, Brian (ed.), *An Autobiography of British Cinema* (London: Methuen/British Film Institute, 1997).

—— *The Encyclopedia of British Film* [2003] (London: Methuen/BFI Publishing, 2nd edn, 2005).

Mousoulis, Bill, 'The Unbearable Lightness of Being: *Wonderland*', *Senses of Cinema*, 7 (2000), www.sensesofcinema.com/contents/00/7/wonderland.html.

Mundy, John, *The British Musical Film* (Manchester: Manchester University Press, 2007)

O'Hagan, Andrew, 'Homing' in Eddie Dick, Andrew Noble and Duncan Petrie (eds), *Bill Douglas: A Lanternist's Account* (London: BFI, 1993), pp. 205–18.

Salwolke, Scott, *Nicolas Roeg: Film by Film* (Jefferson, Nth. Carolina and London: McFarland and Co., 1993).

Schatz, Thomas, *Hollywood Genres* (New York: Random House, 1981).

Sinyard, Neil and Melanie Williams, '"Living in a World That Did Not Want Them": Michael Winterbottom and the Unpopular British Cinema', *Journal of Popular British Cinema*, 5 (2002), pp. 114–23.

Spencer, Liese, 'The Postmodernist Always Wings It Twice', *Sight & Sound*, 2 (2006), pp. 14–17.

Spicer, Andrew, 'British Neo-noir' in Andrew Spicer (ed.), *European Film Noir* (Manchester: Manchester University Press, 2007), pp. 112–37.

Sterne, Laurence, *The Life and Opinions of Tristram Shandy, Gentleman* [1760–67] (Ware, Hertfordshire: Wordsworth Classics, 1996).

Turim, Maureen, *The Films of Oshima Nagisa: Images of a Japanese Iconoclast* (Berkeley, Los Angeles, London: University of California Press, 1998).

Verevis, Constantine, *Film Remakes* (Edinburgh: Edinburgh University Press, 2006).

Wright, Will, *Sixguns & Society: A Structural Study of the Western* (Berkeley et al: University of California Press, 1977).

Index